"Siblings are   tion in *Barbecue*,
Robert O'H   American classic,
or the kind of classic we need."

—*New Yorker*

"This is a look at an America where real-life behaviors take their cues from reality TV . . . *Barbecue* is an examination of a new historical moment, filmed, framed, televised and tweeted, in which everything is in performance."

—*Hollywood Reporter*

"O'Hara has written a comedy about getting reality to fit the truth we've previously constructed for it . . . A meditation on lying and how we all do it when we construct the narratives of 'us.'"

—*NBC*

"O'Hara is a genius at scene-building, that deceptively difficult art of dancing backward and forward at once, and is also inerrant at locating the social experience of his plays at the intersection of voyeurism and minstrelsy . . . A hysterical new play."

—*Vulture*

"A brash, taboo-flouting roast of race and representation."

—*Time Out New York*

"O'Hara has proved he can pull a rabbit out of a hat. *Barbecue* is lousy with rabbits—and laughs . . . There are so many surprises in *Barbecue* that not much can be said about its content without giving them away."

—*Entertainment Weekly*

PRAISE FOR *BOOTYCANDY*

"A searing and sensationally funny comedy about the sometimes poisonous attitude toward homosexuality in black culture . . . *Bootycandy* is as raw in its language and raucous in spirit as it is smart and provocative."

—*New York Times*

"Insanely entertaining . . . *Bootycandy* is basically a spiritual autobiography through satire, loosely tracking the life of a gay black boy named Sutter from childhood through his professional success as a playwright."

—*Vulture*

"Arrestingly original in so many ways . . . O'Hara deliberately walks an uncomfortable line between humor and its opposite, which lends added punch and an air of the unexpected to *Bootycandy*."

—*Boston Globe*

"Funny, smutty and, on the whole, enticingly subversive . . . *Bootycandy* is a toxically satiric portrait of American life, as it is experienced by someone who is black and gay."

—*Washington Post*

"Trashing and lashing out at racial, cultural and sexual stereotypes isn't new. But this vision gets credit for its smarts and unruliness. O'Hara doesn't scrub or sanitize his satire one bit . . . this show is delectably un-PC and potty-mouthed."

—*New York Daily News*

"Largely inspired by writer Robert O'Hara's own experience . . . *Bootycandy* is a raucous romp made up of a series of loosely connected vignettes . . . Sassy, saucy, occasionally graphic and irreverently funny."

—*New York Post*

BARBECUE /
BOOTYCANDY

BOOKS BY ROBERT O'HARA
AVAILABLE FROM TCG

Barbecue / Bootycandy

Insurrection: Holding History

The Fire This Time: African American Plays for the 21st Century
    Edited by Harry J. Elam, Jr. and Robert Alexander
    INCLUDES *Insurrection: Holding History*

BARBECUE / BOOTYCANDY

ROBERT O'HARA

THEATRE COMMUNICATIONS GROUP　　NEW YORK　　2016

Barbecue / Bootycandy is published by Theatre Communications Group, Inc., 520 Eighth Avenue, 24th Floor, New York, NY 10018-4156

The publication of *Barbecue / Bootycandy*, by Robert O'Hara, through TCG's Book Program, is made possible in part by the New York State Council on the Arts with the support of Governor Andrew Cuomo and the New York State Legislature.

TCG books are exclusively distributed to the book trade by Consortium Book Sales and Distribution.

LIBRARY OF CONGRESS CATALOGING-IN-PUBLICATION DATA

O'Hara, Robert, 1970– author. | O'Hara, Robert, 1970– Barbecue.
Bootycandy ; Barbecue / Robert O'Hara.
Other titles: Barbecue.
First edition.
ISBN 9781559364959 (softcover)
ISBN 9781559368049 (ebook)
Subjects: BISAC: DRAMA / American. | SOCIAL SCIENCE / Ethnic Studies / African American Studies.
Classification: LCC PS3565.H296 A6 2016 (print) | LCC PS3565.H296 (ebook)
DDC 812/.54—dc23

Book design and composition by Lisa Govan
Cover design by Jeff Rogers

First Edition, September 2016
Second Printing, November 2021

CONTENTS

PREFACE

Since *Barbecue* and *Bootycandy* are now published in the same book for the first time, I'd like to give a few thoughts that might be helpful for those who take the leap from reading to producing either of these plays.

I encourage you to trust that the "funny" is there. It is built in, and you don't have to play it. Instead, just play the truth.

I think of it this way, if the entirety of the experience is "out of the box," then there is NO "box" from which to come out. I would like to suggest that you "establish the box."

A Normal Box. Pun absolutely intended.

Simple. Honest. Real interactions are what I have tried to craft using a bunch of mixed nuts who think they are as normal as anyone else walking the planet.

There may be a tendency to turn both of these works into *SNL* or *In Living Color* sketches, and while the audience may hoot and holler, they will ultimately miss the painful truth inside both of these pieces. And that truth is, we are all fucked-up.

But fucked-up people rarely believe they are fucked-up . . .

Therefore, let the outrageous live in the language and the given circumstances. Not in the action or design.

Build the box.

Put the play in it.

Watch it break.

—*Robert O'Hara*
July 2016

BARBECUE

To my mother,
Lillie Anne

And her siblings,
James T, Henry, Adlean, Marie, Barbara, T.J.,
Alfonso, Terry, Tyrone, Tina and Melvin

ACKNOWLEDGMENTS

In the scene titled "Alaskan Fishtail," some of the language is lifted from the website for Passages Malibu Alcohol/Drug Rehab: http://www.passagesmalibu.com/

PRODUCTION HISTORY

Barbecue had its world premiere at The Public Theater (Oskar Eustis, Artistic Director; Patrick Willingham, Executive Director) in New York, on October 8, 2015. The play was directed by Kent Gash. The scenic design was by Clint Ramos, the costume design was by Paul Tazewell, the lighting design was by Jason Lyons, the original music and sound design were by Lindsay Jones; the production stage manager was Buzz Cohen. The cast was:

JAMES T	Marc Damon Johnson
	Paul Niebanck
LILLIE ANNE	Becky Ann Baker
	Kim Wayans
ADLEAN	Constance Shulman
	Benja Kay Thomas
MARIE	Arden Myrin
	Heather Alicia Simms
BARBARA	Tamberla Perry
	Samantha Soule

Barbecue was commissioned by Steppenwolf Theatre Company, Chicago (Martha Lavey, Artistic Director; David Hawkansom, Executive Director).

CHARACTERS

JAMES T
LILLIE ANNE
ADLEAN
MARIE
BARBARA

PLACE

Middle America.

SETTING

A pavilion, surrounded by a park.

TIME

Now (after and before).

ACT ONE

ZIPPITY BOOM

James T, a forty/fifty-ish white man, stands speaking on a cell phone.

JAMES T

This is the thing that I don't seem to understand. *WHY?* On God's green earth. Do we still give a damn? No . . . No . . . No . . . No—because it's not about that. You wanna make it about that. But it ain't gonna be about that as long as I'm here. *And I'm here.* Now you gat me out here this morning at the ass crack of dawn to secure this place so I'm *here* . . . And we know she's a fool. We know that she gonna get up in here and act the plum fool . . . Of course she gonna be liquored up. Liquored up. Cracked up. Something upped. She will be upped on something. You know that. I know that. And that's the problem. *Why do we give a damn anymore?* . . . This is not about Mama. Mama didn't give a damn when she was livin and now that she's dead everybody wanna bring her back up out the grave to say what the hell she would do if she was here. She ain't here. She dead.

And she didn't give a damn about Barbara's bullshit so don't try and make it out like she would give a damn now. She dead. Let the heifa stay dead . . . Taking it easy? What? Who the hell are *you* talking about? I'm talking about *Barbara*. Zippity Boom. Our sister. Remember her? She don't know from no gatdamn "taking it easy." She gat two modes. *Zippity. Boom.* Ain't shit in between. Ain't no zippity-do-dah. When she taste liquor. She go *Zippity. Boom!* Period. I know it. You know it. And any fool who knows anything about Barbara knows it. See yall wanna sit back today and act like we a normal gatdamn family. We ain't no normal gatdamn family and we ain't never been no normal gatdamn family but all of a sudden yall read a book or see a TV show and yall wanna *gather* up and act like we a normal gatdamn family. Zippity Boom is gonna walk up in here and act out her head— Barbara don't give a damn about us all being here. Why should she give a damn about that? And how you gonna keep liquor away from Barbara?— *She wake up high!!!* Zippity Boom will roll up in here and it will be a *wrap*. We might as well draw three gatdamn circles pitch a tent and hand out tickets because when ZIPPITY BOOM rolls up into this heah park its gonna be the Greatest Show on the muthafuckin Earth.

(He looks off.)

Is that you riding up?

(He waves.)

Yeah . . . this me waving.

(He clicks his cell phone off. Then he goes to a cooler and takes out a beer and drinks.
Soon, Lillie Anne comes onstage. She is fifty/sixty-ish and white.)

LILLIE ANNE

Hey there.

(James T says nothing. He just stares at her and continues drinking his beer.)

What? . . . Do these shorts make me look fat?

JAMES T

Naw, yo fat makes you look fat.

LILLIE ANNE

Shut up James T and come help me—

JAMES T

Don't shut up James T and come help me *nuthin*. Lillie Anne, I been tellin you for the last month that I didn't want to be here today so I'm not planning to help do *nuthin*.

LILLIE ANNE

You *are* here and I need your help now get up and *help me* bring some of this stuff up here so we can start decoratin—

JAMES T

Decoratin?

LILLIE ANNE

We gotta make it look like something don't we?

JAMES T

We ain't gotta make it look like *nuthin* . . . I ain't decoratin—

LILLIE ANNE

She has to believe it's a gatdamn party otherwise what the hell is the use?

JAMES T

That's exactly my gatdamn question. What the hell is the use?

LILLIE ANNE

She's our sister.

JAMES T

She's a gatdamn waste of—

LILLIE ANNE

James T I'm not gonna dance with you over this all day today.
Now if you want a pat on your gatdamn back for comin today
then come on over here and I will pat you on your gatdamn
back but I don't have the energy nor the interest in rustlin and
tumblin with you over being here. You and me both know you
ain't gat nuthin else to do this morning and therefore the least
you can achieve in your trailer park living asshole of a life is to
help your sister in her time of need.

JAMES T

I gat four sisters in a time of need one of which is you.

LILLIE ANNE

I'm talking about the sister with the crack habit.

JAMES T

I gat two of those.

LILLIE ANNE

I'm talking bout the one with the crack habit and the alcohol
problem.

JAMES T

And two of those.

LILLIE ANNE

The one with the crack habit, alcohol problem and the mental
illness.

JAMES T

Fuck her.

LILLIE ANNE

Too late. Life done already done that.

(A car beeps from off.
  They both look.)

JAMES T

What the—???

LILLIE ANNE

I know she did not bring them badass— *(Shouting off)* ADLEAN, I KNOW YOU DIDN'T BRING THEM BADASS GRAND-KIDS AFTER I TOLD YOU NOT TO BRING THEM NASTY GOOD FOR NUTHIN BADASS— *KEEP THEM GATDAMN GRANDKIDS IN THAT GATDAMN CAR!! (To James T)* They wanna get my pressure goin.

(Two forty/fifty-ish white women enter. They are Adlean, who carries a carton of menthol cigarettes, and Marie, who carries a large bottle of Jack Daniels.)

MARIE

(To Lillie Anne) Why you screamin so gatdamn loud this early in the mornin Lillie Anne?

ADLEAN

Hey there James T, how that cancer in your balls doin?

JAMES T

I guess about the same as that cancer in that one good titty you gat left.

LILLIE ANNE

Adlean, didn't I tell you not to come bringin them gatdamn badass grandkids of yours?

MARIE

(Regarding the Jack Daniels) Where the cups at?

11

ADLEAN

They stayin in the car is that a problem for you or should I just bag them back into the street and have them play in traffic?

JAMES T

You should have left them wherever the hell they woke up this gatdamn morning.

LILLIE ANNE

This ain't no damn place for no gatdamn grandkids.

MARIE

It's a gatdamn park ain't it?

LILLIE ANNE

Today. It ain't. Today. We gat important business to attend to and we don't need no damn badass—

ADLEAN

(Yelling off) BOOTY IF YOU DON'T STOP BOPPIN YO HEAD UP IN AND OUT OF MY GATDAMN SUNROOF I'M GONNA COME OVER THERE AND SLAP THE FUCK OUT OF YOU WITH A HAMMER TILL YOUR THROAT CLAP!

LILLIE ANNE

Adlean—

ADLEAN

(Still shouting off) AND I MEANS THAT! I'LL BEAT YOU TILL I SEE THE WHITE MEAT. (Now back to the others) Stupid-ass fool.

MARIE

I told you he gonna need somethin stronger than them gatdamn Ritalins.

ADLEAN

He eat that shit like it's cornflakes.

JAMES T

You break a tire iron over his gatdamn forehead and them Ritalins might take hold.

LILLIE ANNE

Could we all take a moment. And shut the hell up.

(Silence.)

Thank you. Now. I gat some stuff in my car that I need yall to help me take out and bring up here to cook and decorate.

MARIE AND ADLEAN

Decorate?

LILLIE ANNE

Yes! Decorate! We have to make this look like a real party or it will not work. She won't even get out the car if she don't believe it's a real party.

ADLEAN

(Skeptical) So you bought real food?

(Silence. Lillie Anne looks at Adlean like she's crazy.)

LILLIE ANNE

Naw I went to the *fake* grocery store and bought some *fake* food, what the hell do you think, heifa?

MARIE

Where the mixers and cups at?

LILLIE ANNE

I just told you, Marie, I have everything in my car gaddammit, and I need you all to—

*(Marie turns and walks off toward the car.
Silence.)*

(Referring to Marie) Now pretty soon, that Jack Daniels will start talking for that heifa. And she won't be of no damn use. I want Barbara to see just that.

ADLEAN

Why?

JAMES T

So she'll think it's a *real* gatdamn family event.

LILLIE ANNE

Exactly. Now James T. I gat a bunch of stuff for the grill so I will need you to get on that. Adlean you can help me blow up the balloons and put up the party favors and Marie—

MARIE

(From off) WHY THE HELL IS YOUR DOORS LOCKED IF YOU WANT US TO HELP YOU OUT SO GATDAMN MUCH!!!

LILLIE ANNE

Marie will drink and let that Jack start talking.

ADLEAN

You really expect Barbara to show up?

JAMES T

That's *my* next question.

LILLIE ANNE

Fonzi is bringing her.

JAMES T

Fonzi???

ADLEAN

When he get out of jail?

LILLIE ANNE

Fonzi been out of jail for a year and half now.

JAMES T

Where the hell he been at?

LILLIE ANNE

He been staying away from the family hoping to get his life back together.

ADLEAN

What he gat to stay away from the family for that for?

JAMES T

That asshole owe me twenty dollars.

ADLEAN

Twenty dollars? That asshole owe me fifty.

(Marie reenters.)

MARIE

(To Lillie Anne) Heifa where your keys at?

LILLIE ANNE

(Handing her the keys) Here.

ADLEAN

Fonzi is out. Been out for a year n half!

MARIE

What??!! That asshole owe me seventy-five *dollars*!

LILLIE ANNE

Fonzi thought it would be best if he kept himself away from up under our influence while he lived in his sober house and—

ADLEAN

From up under OUR influence?

LILLIE ANNE

Yes.

MARIE

Correct me if I'm mistaken but ain't *he* the one they had to mount a manhunt for ten years ago?

LILLIE ANNE

He thinks it's better to—

JAMES T

Better to just contact *you* cuz you the one that likes to keep secrets and shit. How the hell you got him *driving* Barbara over here?

MARIE

Fonzi ain't gat no license, Lillie Anne.

ADLEAN

(To Lillie Anne) He's a felon, don't you know that?

LILLIE ANNE

(Fed up) Of course I know he's a gatdamn felon! But he's out. And he's bringing her. And we are not here to figure out who owes who what from ten gatdamn years ago. We are here for Barbara. Our sister. Zippity Boom. We are here for her. Everybody knows, a barbecue is her favorite type of party. And this is her favorite park. Now when the time is just right. When she is safe and comfortable. In the bosom of her loving brother and sisters. And the heifa can't see what's coming. We will start the fucking intervention.

(Black.)

JACK TALKIN

James T, Lillie Anne, Adlean and Marie are all now played by black actors.

They are in the same costumes as the white actors from the last scene.

It is VERY IMPORTANT that there be no *attempt to make either cast look (physically) like the other, besides wearing the same costumes.*

Therefore, the ages of the black cast are irrelevant.

The BBQing and decorating are now in full swing.

James T is turning meat on the grill and drinking a beer.

Adlean is blowing up balloons with PARTY words on them in between popping pills and chain smoking.

Lillie Anne is laying out tablecloths and utensils and the like while also texting on her smartphone.

Marie, loud and loaded, drinks from a big red plastic cup full of ice and Jack Daniels. She does nothing else besides stand around talking shit.

MARIE

(*Loud drunk*) . . . that's what I'm trying to tell you. It was me, Tina, Tyrone, Melvin, Terry and Alphonso.

ADLEAN

Melvin whatn't there.

JAMES T

He was there.

ADLEAN

I'm telling you Melvin whatn't there. He was locked up with Henry and Junior.

JAMES T

(*To Adlean*) What the hell you talking about, Adlean?

MARIE

Adlean, *you* wasn't even there so how the hell you know who was where?

LILLIE ANNE

(*To Adlean*) *Melvin was there.*

ADLEAN

How the hell you know? You didn't show up until after ME?

LILLIE ANNE

I know because *Melvin* was the one who called *me*.

ADLEAN

I don't remember seeing Melvin.

MARIE

And what the hell that gat to do with anything. You probably don't even remember waking up this morning with all them damn pills you poppin.

ADLEAN

Heifa, you wait till you get you a disease in *yo* titty—

MARIE

I was the one who told you not to go eating no damn corn out no damn can. It's them damn canned goods that gave you that damn cancer.

LILLIE ANNE

Marie shut the hell up.

MARIE

I'm telling the truth. They put that damn cancer in all these damn canned goods.

JAMES T

Who the hell put it in there Marie?

MARIE

Them damn Middle Easterners.

ADLEAN

How the hell do Middle Easterners put cancer in a damn canned good Marie?

MARIE

I don't know! How the hell did they blow up 9/11?

(Silence.)

LILLIE ANNE

Marie, help do something and be quiet.

MARIE

Yall don't want to believe me but that's the damn honest to God truth.

JAMES T

We don't get canned goods or CORN from no damn Middle
Easterners.

MARIE

Who you think *own* the damn grocery stores?? HUH? And *why*
when I pick up my phone to call somebody for help for something they sound like they in the gatdamn MIDDLE of the
gatdamn Middle East.

LILLIE ANNE

They in India fool. They ain't in no gatdamn Middle East.

ADLEAN

They ain't even gat no phones in no damn Middle East. You
just like making shit up.

MARIE

Alright. Yall believe what yall want but I don't eat no damn
canned goods and I ain't gat no damn cancer so the proof is in
the damn puddin.

JAMES T

No the proof is in that damn Jack Daniels you slurpin.

MARIE

Anyway as I was saying, it was me, Tina, Tyrone, Melvin and
Terry—

ADLEAN

Melvin whatn't—

JAMES T AND LILLIE ANNE

Yes he was!!

MARIE

We was all at the house on Baltimore. And Mama had just started batterin some chicken and Big Bob came runnin in shoutin—"HE KILLED MAMA HE KILLED MAMA!" And I was like, "WHO KILLED WHO??!!" And Big Bob was like, "WHOOKIE JUST KILLED MAMA!!" Then all of a sudden the rest of Big Bob's brothers and sisters come running into the damn house with blood all over their arms and stuff and I'm like, "WAIT A GATDAMN MINUTE WHAT'S GOIN ONS???" *(Laughing)* And they all started talkin real fast real quick and we all ran out to the porch and they pointed across the street at their house and—

LILLIE ANNE

Why are you laughing???

MARIE

(Simply) . . . It was funny. *(Beat)* So of course me, Tina, Tyrone, *MELVIN*, Terry and Alphonso, we take our curious asses on over there to see what was what and when we get there we walk into the kitchen and see Whookie standing there smoking a cigarette with his mama's head *sitting* on the counter next to him . . . Her *body* on the floor and her *head* on the counter. Blood everywhere . . . and Whookie was real cool just talking to her like ain't nothing was nothing. "I told you to give me a gatdamn cigarette. I ain't gat time for no damn games Mama. Now you see. *Now* you see. All you have to do is give me a gatdamn cigarette and we be cool." This crazy fool chopped his own mama's head off cuz she refused to give him her last damn cigarette. Yall remember.

LILLIE ANNE

Of course we remember. Every time you tell this damn story we remember.

ADLEAN

I really don't remember Melvin being out of jail when that happened . . .

LILLIE ANNE

I told you Melvin called me and told me to get over there and I called you.

ADLEAN

I remember you calling me but—

MARIE

It's them *GATDAMN* pills they gat you on, I told you, you don't need all them damn pills!!! That's how folks lose time and shit and who you think run them damn doctor offices and them damn pill companies?

JAMES T

The Middle Easterners?

MARIE

You damn skippy. They gat all that shit on lock. Trust me.

JAMES T

What the hell is your point Marie.

MARIE

What the hell is my point?

JAMES T

Yes. Your point. What the hell is it?

MARIE

My point is that yall know that Barbara has been *known* for carrying razor blades between her teeth.

(Silence.

Lillie Anne, James T and Adlean look to each other knowing the Jack Daniels has truly set in.)

LILLIE ANNE

Barbara gat dentures, fool.

ADLEAN

What?

LILLIE ANNE

Barbara's teeth fell out five years ago and the doctor gave her dentures? How the hell she gon carry razor blades *AND* dentures in her mouth at the same damn time?

ADLEAN

I didn't know about all that.

JAMES T

From all that damn shit she been doin. Rotted her damn teeth clean out her damn mouth.

MARIE

That heifa has been *KNOWN*!! . . . Do yall hear me! Check her record! She has been *KNOWN* for carrying razor blades between her damn gums or teeth or dentures or something.

LILLIE ANNE

That was just that *one time* and they couldn't prove it!

MARIE

(Gone) That bitch threw some *Poligrip* up into her gatdamn mouth, slapped some razor blades between her gums and when they caught Zippity Boom, she had on a halter top and som apple bottom shorts. She said a couple of wimmen jumped her. One held her hands behind her back and the other was beatin her upside her face. Barbara pushed that damn razor blade to

the front of her damn mouth and sliced the both of them up. *Zippity Boom is baddd. She. Do. Not. Play.*

LILLIE ANNE

. . . And?

MARIE

And??? . . . And??? . . . I just told you she carry *razor blades in her in damn mouth* and you sayin AND???

ADLEAN

So you think she might get violent?

MARIE

Zippity Boom climbs out jailhouse windows and beats up grown-ass niggas with bats. YES! I think she might get violent.

JAMES T

She right. Zippity Boom just might get violent and we need to be prepared for just that. That's why I brought along this.

(He takes out a taser.
   Silence.)

ADLEAN

Is that a taser?

JAMES T

Naw it's a glass of lemonade.

LILLIE ANNE

Where the hell did you—

JAMES T

Don't worry about it.

MARIE

This ain't Iraq put that shit—

JAMES T

The minute Zippity Boom get out of hand this will calm her back down.

LILLIE ANNE

She gat a bad heart!

JAMES T

Then she better stay calm.

ADLEAN

I don't think Barbara is going to get violent. I don't think she will even be coming today.

MARIE

Zippity Boom can smell free liquor within ten square blocks. If Fonzi can get her within them ten square blocks then Zippity Boom will be here.

LILLIE ANNE

You brought a taser to your sister's intervention, James T?

JAMES T

And I gat some gatdamn rope and duct tape in the glove compartment of my gatdamn car.

LILLIE ANNE

This has to be *voluntary* fool. The whole point is that we tell her how much we love her and how much we want our real sister back and stuff.

ADLEAN

(*Mocking*) And stuff.

JAMES T

And after we tell her all *that* bullshit and she starts to buck up like the gorilla that she is, then I'll have to put her down.

LILLIE ANNE

James T—

JAMES T

I told you that I didn't want to come messin with Barbara this morning!!!

ADLEAN

She ain't coming so yall wasting yall gatdamn breath!

LILLIE ANNE

(To Adlean) Could you be just a little bit optimistic! This is suppose to be a gatdamn *intervention* and we need a *little bit* of optimism for it work!

MARIE

She on CRACK, Lillie Anne!

LILLIE ANNE

YOU'RE ON CRACK, MARIE!

(Silence.)

That's right. We know all about it.

(Silence.)

MARIE

Yall don't know *all* about *nuthin*.

LILLIE ANNE

James T??

JAMES T

Adlean told me she found—

ADLEAN

(Lying) I never told you *nuthin* don't go putting my name—

JAMES T

You told me you found some stuff in her purse last week.

MARIE

Last week?

ADLEAN

(Lying) I never said—

MARIE

What the hell you going through my purse for, Adlean?

ADLEAN

What the hell you doing crack for, Marie?

(Beat.)

LILLIE ANNE

You've seen what it's done to our family.

MARIE

I ain't like Barbara. Zippity Boom has always been a gatdamn glutton.

LILLIE ANNE

It's CRACK, Marie!

JAMES T

After Tina and Henry and now Barbara, how could you be stupid enough to get anywhere near that shit?!

MARIE

You of all gatdamn people ain't gat no room to talk, James T.

ADLEAN

Marie you left your purse in my bathroom last week and I wasn't even trying to look into it—

MARIE

But you did. You did. Nosy heifa. How you know it was mine? Huh? See you know so damn much how you know the crack was mine?

LILLIE ANNE

It was in your purse!

MARIE

There's a lot of shit in my purse that ain't mine!!

JAMES T

Go open your purse.

MARIE

I ain't going to open *nuthin*. This ain't my intervention. And you ain't my daddy.

ADLEAN

If you want us to believe you then you have to go open your purse and—

MARIE

I don't have to go do *nuthin* but stay black and die.

LILLIE ANNE

Is that what you want?

ADLEAN

You want to die, Marie?

MARIE

Whose gatdamn intervention is this??!!

LILLIE ANNE

We're not trying to do no damn intervention on you. We just want you to know that *we know*! And if Barbara can get some help then maybe you need to think about it as well.

MARIE

I don't need—

JAMES T, ADLEAN AND LILLIE ANNE

Negro, please.

MARIE

And how many beers is that for you James T? You smell like a gatdamn discount liquor outlet. And to top that off you're HIGH as a kite. Should we *interview intervene invoke* on yo weed-tokin broke ass? And you Adlean, how many gatdamn painkillers did you throw down your gatdamn throat since you been sitting up in here? Let's get yo oxycodone perc-a-muth-afuckin-set ass an intervention up in this heah park. And Lillie Anne you're the worst of all. You like putting shit together sittin yo fat ass up on your high horse telling everybody else what the hell is wrong with they lives. Well grab a gatdamn mirror and a notepad cuz yo ass—

(James T shocks Marie with the taser.
She freaks out. Foams at the mouth. And falls to the ground.
Adlean and Lillie Anne look at him like he's gone crazy. Then they slowly go back to doing whatever they were doing.
Silence.)

JAMES T

. . . Now that's set on low. Barbara will probably need it set to medium-high if she go Zippity Boom. But I'll be ready for her.

(He turns meat on the grill and continues to drink his beer.
Black.)

ALASKAN FISHTAIL

White cast.

Lillie Anne (texting) and Adlean (smoking and popping pills) look at Marie who is on the ground, slowly recovering from the shock of the taser.

Soon Marie stumbles to her feet and pours some more Jack Daniels into her big red plastic cup full of ice.

James T drinks a beer, still turning meat.

After a moment:

MARIE

What the hell happened?

(Lillie Anne and Adlean look to James T. Then:)

ADLEAN

(To Marie) You blacked out.

MARIE

I blacked out?

LILLIE ANNE

That damn Jack gat to talking and you blacked out.

MARIE

How long was I out?

LILLIE ANNE

. . . Bout ten minutes.

ADLEAN

You were talking all that stuff about canned goods and—

MARIE

And I blacked out.

JAMES T

. . . Yup.

(Silence.)

MARIE

And none of yall thought to help me up off the gatdamn ground??

(Silence.)

ADLEAN

We figured you could use the rest.

LILLIE ANNE

Let the liquor get outta your system and stuff.

MARIE

(Drinking) All I remember is everything just went . . . Black.

JAMES T

Well . . . that there would be the definition . . . of a blackout . . .

(Silence. She looks to each of them with suspicion.
    Sound of a text message.)

LILLIE ANNE

(Referring to the text) Alright!! Fonzi says they're ten minutes away. Does everybody have their letters?

MARIE

What letters?

LILLIE ANNE

Gatdammit I *told* you we were all suppose to write a letter that we read to her and after every letter that person is suppose to ask her to go to—

ADLEAN

Wait a second. You already lost me. We read her a letter and then *ask* her something?

LILLIE ANNE

Ask her to go to rehab. To get help.

JAMES T

I keep trying to tell you that Zippity Boom don't want no help.

LILLIE ANNE

We ask her. Over and over. After each letter. Only she can't answer.

ADLEAN

She can't answer.

LILLIE ANNE

No. She has to wait until everybody is done with their letters and when everybody has asked her to go to rehab, over and over, *then* she can answer. So it's about the *accumulation* of our outpouring of love. We are asking her to make the choice to start the first day of her life again.

(Silence.
      They all just look at Lillie Anne.)

So who remembered to write a letter to read?

(James T, Marie and Adlean are silent.)

Useless . . . All of you . . . Useless.

ADLEAN

This yo thang you runnin it. So run it.

LILLIE ANNE

Yall just gon have to speak from the gatdamn heart then.

MARIE

What the hell does that mean?

LILLIE ANNE

Speak your truth.

ADLEAN

And what the hell does *that* mean?

JAMES T

It means you should tell Zippity Boom to put the gatdamn crack pipe down and get some gatdamn help.

LILLIE ANNE

It *means* . . . you need to tell Barbara what *she* means to *you*. She needs to know we are here to support her and *not* to make her feel bad or nuthin, just because she's a crackhead. Speak about how we all use to have so much fun with her when we was young, James T, how you use to put her on your shoulders and take her to the penny candy store, and Adlean how she would brighten up your day with the way she always came into your room and tickled your feet in the morning, and Marie how she use to lay in the grass with you and you all would look up at the stars counting the constellations until Mama would call you in for dinner and on the way in you and Barbara would catch fireflies and how we all use to use them as night lights stuck in a jar when we slept outside in that ole tent in the backyard next to that ole swing set.

(Pause.)

MARIE

So lie to her.

LILLIE ANNE

Yes. Lie to the heifa. Barbara don't remember shit about her childhood anyway.

JAMES T

What happens when she tells us to go fuck ourselves and stay out her gatdamn life.

LILLIE ANNE

Ignore it.

ADLEAN

Ignore it.

LILLIE ANNE

Ignore it.

MARIE

And you've seen this work before?

LILLIE ANNE

Works all the time on TV.

ADLEAN

Are you talking about that show where they chase them folks out into the streets yelling at them to please go get some help and stuff?

LILLIE ANNE

Yes. And on that show, the crackheads always cuss and fuss and stomp and shout but if you keep after them they will eventually say yes. We just might have to wrestle Zippity Boom down with *love*.

MARIE

So we suppose to chase Barbara around this park begging her to go to rehab?

LILLIE ANNE

If we have to.

ADLEAN

I'm not chasing *nobody* around this big ass park, I gat cancer in my titty, I can't be chasing folks around parks.

JAMES T

Say she agrees.

MARIE

Which she won't.

ADLEAN

Of course she won't.

JAMES T

But say she does.

LILLIE ANNE

She will.

JAMES T

Say we win the lotto and we look up and pigs are flying and Zippity Boom decides to go to rehab. Then what?

LILLIE ANNE

I have it all set up.

ADLEAN

You have it all set up.

LILLIE ANNE

There is a place waiting for her. They are expecting her within the next twenty-four hours. It's called Halcyon Dreams. The plane ticket has already been bought.

ADLEAN

The plane ticket has already been—

LILLIE ANNE

Bitch, is your name *Echo*?!! Yes a plane ticket! She can't WALK to *Alaska* can she?

(Silence.
    James T, Adlean and Marie all look at Lillie Anne as if she's lost her mind.
    Then:)

ADLEAN

Alaska?

LILLIE ANNE

Yes! I've *researched*!

MARIE

What *research*?!!

(Beat.

Lillie Anne goes over to her purse and rifles through it. Soon she retrieves a colorful brochure.)

LILLIE ANNE

See here! Halcyon Dreams Alcohol Rehab and Drug Addiction Treatment!

(Marie snatches the brochure.)

MARIE

(Reading) . . . *Psycho*therapy?
    Acupuncture and Acupressure?
    Massage??
    Hypnotherapy?
    Equine Assisted Therapy??

JAMES T

What the hell is that?

MARIE

(Continuing) Spiritual Counseling?
    The Ropes Course?
    YOGA!!??

LILLIE ANNE

Yes *yoga*!

MARIE

How the hell you gonna send somebody all the way out to Alaska for *yoga*??!!

(James T takes the brochure and reads.)

JAMES T

(Reading) "With *Equine* Assisted Therapy, rather than talking to a therapist, you and others interact with a *horse*."

(Silence.)

(To Lillie Anne) Is this som joke?

LILLIE ANNE

No. It ain't no damn joke.

ADLEAN

Yoga and *horses*.

LILLIE ANNE

Yes *yoga* and *horses*.

MARIE

And *massages*! And *acupuncture* and *acupressure*!

(Adlean takes the brochure from James T.)

LILLIE ANNE

It's all a part of her *treatment*.

ADLEAN

(Reading) Hypnotherapy . . . your therapist will tap into any feelings of anger, fear, anxiety, sadness, or pain that you may have? *(To Lillie Anne)* Barbara ain't gat none of that. *(Reading)* "The Ropes Course."

JAMES T

Zippity Boom ain't gonna climb no rope.

ADLEAN

(Reading) "The Ropes Course is a fun, safe yet challenging personal growth and team-building activity in a beautiful setting,

but it also helps our clients meet a number of goals by focusing on personal achievements . . ." *(To Lillie Anne)* Barbara ain't got no *personal achievements.*

JAMES T

(Disgust) Yoga. Horses. Massages. Hypnosis. And *ropes.*

MARIE

(Disgust) In *Alaska.*

ADLEAN

(Disgust) And *this* is your *research.*

(Silence.
Lillie Anne just looks at them all.
Then:)

LILLIE ANNE

(Calmly) . . . May I have that brochure back now please?

(Pause.
Adlean hands her the brochure.
Lillie Anne calmly looks over the brochure, then begins to read.)

(Calmly) "The Philosophy of Halcyon Dreams."
   (She looks to her family, then reads) "We do not believe that drug and alcohol dependency is a disease. Instead, we believe your addiction is the result of four causes of dependency, which are—

(A car beeps from far off.)

(Looking off) That's them.

(She waves off. She puts the brochure away.)

Music!

(She races to an iPod speaker hookup and turns on music.

She abruptly turns to the others who stand looking at her like she is crazy.)

Dance, gatdammit!

(James T, Marie and Adlean reluctantly start dancing.)

(Shaking her hips) Listen all of you. Do Not Mention ALASKA to Zippity Boom. Period. She don't need to know where the hell she's going.

MARIE

She's gonna ask.

LILLIE ANNE

Let her.

ADLEAN

Wait a second.

LILLIE ANNE

What!!

ADLEAN

You really expect us to try and get Zippity Boom on a plane to *ALASKA*??

LILLIE ANNE

It needed to be some place that she couldn't escape on foot. She can't hitchhike back from Alaska so gatdamn easy.

JAMES T

She will surely try.

LILLIE ANNE

I've told them all about Zippity Boom's tendencies.

MARIE

Have you told them about them damn razor blades in her gatdamn mouth tendencies?

LILLIE ANNE

(Looking off but speaking to the others) They're parking.

(She motions for them to "party."
They all "party," laugh.
It begins to feel rather genuine.
This is a family that knows how to LIE. Together.
They dance with abandon.
Soon:)

JAMES T

How long do we have to keep this shit up?

LILLIE ANNE

I will give a signal for when the intervention is to begin.

ADLEAN

And what will that be?

LILLIE ANNE

The fishtail dance.

MARIE

(Stops dancing) So we wait until Barbara starts doing the fishtail
dance then we—

LILLIE ANNE

No! When *I* start doing the fishtail dance then we'll—

JAMES T

(Stops dancing) Why would you ever do the gatdamn fishtail
dance?

MARIE

You know you can't dance worth *nuthin* Lillie Anne.

LILLIE ANNE

So what! The signal will be the FISHTAIL DANCE!!

ADLEAN

(Stops dancing) Then the gig will be UP because you can't do the fishtail dance for shit.

LILLIE ANNE

You know what? Fuck you Adlean.

ADLEAN

No you know *what*? Fuck you Lillie Anne. I'm just trying to give some constructive criticism cause you ain't the only one up in here with a GED.

LILLIE ANNE

Don't start with me yall just be ready for when I bend over and do the gatdamn fishtail dance, that's the signal for everybody to stop whatever the hell they doing—

JAMES T

And do what? Laugh???

MARIE

Cuz that's what we usually do when we see you trying to do the fishtail dance.

ADLEAN

So we should just change the signal to when everybody starts laughing at your dumb ass trying to do the fishtail dance.

(Barbara, a mid-thirties/forties white woman enters while Lillie Anne speaks. Lillie Anne is oblivious of Barbara's presence.)

LILLIE ANNE

(Stops dancing) I don't give a hot googolie gatdamn who laughs as long as we can get Barbara's stupid ass onto that damn plane tonight to the rehab!

You can laugh all damn day if you like just don't mention shit about where it's at or start acting like this FAKE-ASS barbecue is really a gatdamn INTERVENTION until I give you the Fishtail Dance Signal!!!

(She turns and sees that Barbara is standing next to her and has heard everything.

Silence. Except for the music. Then:

Lillie Anne puts her hands behind her back, bends over and begins to dance the fishtail.

Black.)

INTERVENTION

Black cast.

    Barbara is bound and gagged with rope and duct-taped to a supporting pillar/column.

    James T holds his taser as he speaks.

JAMES T

. . . And I remember the time. I use to put you on my shoulders and we'd go down to the penny candy store. And you'd get them Lemonheads. And them Red Hots. And mix them together. Once they were good and soggy in your mouth you'd open up wide and stick your tongue out and laugh. You called it pink lemonade. I miss that sister, Barbara. The one that useta catch fireflies with me at night and useta use them as night lights stuck in a jar when we slept outside in that ole tent in the backyard next to that ole swing set. I miss the way as you gat older you'd call me and we'd talk about Eric and Peanut and all those men who ever tried to hurt you. And you'd say, "Brotha I need your help." Once or twice I'd come over there and hold one of them down while you beat the hell out of em with a brick. I want that sister back. That's the sister I want back.

(Suddenly very emotional) . . . You been on this a long time Barbara. And Sis it's time to let it go. It's time to let it go Zippity Boom. And come on home. Go get the help we're offering you and come on home. We need you to let it go Barbara. Get the help. Will you do this? Will you take this opportunity that we are offering to you? And come on home.

(Silence.

The bound and gagged Barbara makes no gesture of speech or movement.)

LILLIE ANNE

(Softly) Alright, Adlean. Now you.

(Adlean looks to Lillie Anne and doesn't move.)

(Softly) Go on. Tell her what you have on your heart.

(Slowly, Adlean steps closer.)

ADLEAN

. . . Barbara . . . I remember how you use to come in and . . . tickle my feet in the morning. You knew I never liked getting up for school so you said you'd wake me up with a laugh. And I know sometimes I'd bust you in the jaw with a shoe . . . but the ticklin grew on me and I started to expect it . . . Well Barbara . . . I need my little tickle alarm clock back in my life. I would like to leave this earth knowing that you had gotten your life back together . . . put yourself together in a whole different way without all those drugs and drink. It makes me very sad to have to be riding through downtown with my grandkids and see you standing on the street corner after having shitted on yourself. That one time I stopped . . . it broke my heart to see you. But you should know I have not stopped many many many times Barbara. The time you were riding on the front of that old man's Hoveround wheelchair. In the middle of the street. The time you were chasing down some wimmen with a hot glue gun and no draws on your ass. Ass just in the air. In the middle of the street. I said to myself, "Is that my sister Barbara? In the middle of the gatdamn street?" . . . I don't stop anymore. For the sake of my grandkids I don't stop. But Zippity Boom *you* have to stop. *You* need help, Barbara. We've found a place that can help you. We will be here to support you when you return. Barbara, will you please take this gift we are giving you. We love you. Will you please go to rehab, Barbara? Will you please take this help from those nice people up there in Alaska?

(Suddenly Barbara moves on the word "Alaska."
    The others glare at Adlean, who covers her mouth with her hands.
    Silence.)

LILLIE ANNE

(To Marie through clenched teeth) Marie.

(Marie keeps her distance from Barbara.)

MARIE

. . . Barbara . . . Zippity Boom . . .
    (Sings) "Sistah you been on my mind" . . . *(Beat)* You remember when you and me and Lillie Anne and Adlean and Tina we all went out and had us a girl's night out?

ADLEAN

Tina whatn't there.

(They all glare at Adlean again, who again covers her mouth.)

MARIE

(Back to Barbara) . . . We went to that little club downtown on the corner of Grafton. What was it called? I think it was Kellers. Remember. We had to sneak Tina in cuz she had just turned sixteen or something. We all sat up in there like we was grown and dared anybody to tell us any different . . . You had your first piña colada. And we could tell you liked it. Cuz that was the day we met Zippity Boom. Zippity Boom-Boom. She came OUT that night for the first time and we was all laughing. We use to *laugh*, Barbara. Remember. Just all night. Remember when we gat back from Kellers that night . . . we snuck in through the side window and we had to almost smother you to keep you from laughing too loud and waking up Mama and Daddy . . . and we all just decided to sleep in the same bed . . . *sistahs* . . . *togetha* . . . We woke up just like that in the morning . . . *togetha* . . . *woke up* . . . from a bucket of ice cold water being thrown on us . . . looked down and saw that we were all tied to one another remember? Mama standing there . . . empty bucket in one hand and in the other hand she had that green water hose she had cut in half . . . Remember that . . . that green snake whip . . . She proceeded to beat the hell out of all of us . . . and you . . . Zippity Boom . . . you just kept right on laughing . . . I want my sister back . . . I want my sister that can take an ass-beating and laugh through that shit . . . I want you to get help Barbara . . . Please will you go?

(Silence.
Lillie Anne steps forward.)

LILLIE ANNE

. . . I'm sorry I lied to you, Barbara. I'm sorry I had to have Fonzi lie to you as well. I'm sorry he had to leave immediately and not explain himself but his parole requires that he not be around alcohol, drugs or firearms. Most of all I'm sorry we've had to bring you out in the public like this.

(Lillie Anne pulls out a piece of paper from her bosom.)

(Reading) "Barbara. The truth is. Nobody wanted you in their house to tear up their shit during this intervention. And that's a shame Barbara. It's a shame when your own family don't trust you or want you near any of their shit . . . Barbara you are a thief and liar and the truth ain't in ya. So today we bring you here. To this barbecue party in your favorite park. To perform this intervention. *To step in*. Today we finally *step in*. As a family. To encircle you with truth and love. In the open air. In the open air Barbara, my sweet sistah we encircle you *TODAY* with truth and love!!"

(She takes a moment to gather herself, then continues to read.)

"Barbara. I don't like that I have to be your SSI payee. You came to me. You confided in me that you were going to be getting disability. But they wouldn't give *you* the check. They told you that you had to have a payee. And you *confided* in me that you didn't trust any of these other fools up in this family with your money. And you wanted me to be your payee. When I asked you what disability you had, Barbara, you said, "Lillie Anne. I'm on crack." And I said, "When did that become a disability." But I see now Barbara. You. Are. Disabled. We have *enabled* you to become *disabled*. Well today Barbara. *We step in*. Starting from *TODAY*. You will no longer be allowed to call upon any of us. To ask any of us to come pick you up.

Give you a few dollars for a beer or a pack of cigarettes. To come help you get Eric's fingers from around your throat. To come help you get Peanut and his other whores out of your house after another weekend junkie convention in your living room."

(Everybody begins to look at Lillie Anne like she's gone crazy.)

"If you do not take this gift of *new hope* we are offering and go to the rehab, I will no longer be your payee, Barbara. I will proceed to rip up every single gatdamn check from SSI that comes to my house for you. If you do not take this gift of *new life* that we are offering you, I will pull out my gatdamn cell phone right here and now and dial the police and have them come here *immediately* to arrest you for whatever shit you have on you at this moment. I will tell them that it was indeed you who took a sledge hammer to the door of the first grade class of North Fairmount Elementary School last month and stole their DVD player for crack. I will call the fire department and report that the arson last year on Eric's car, was indeed set by you and Eric for insurance money for crack and all they have to do is look at the scars on his back because both of you were too stupid to get the hell out of the way of the gatdamn flames. I will call the FBI and notify them that Peanut is the leading child pornographer in this city and he sometimes stays at your home. They will proceed to raid your apartment and take everything you have in it out for evidence. I will then proceed to—"

JAMES T

Gatdamn you gon do all *that*???

LILLIE ANNE

Yes.

ADLEAN

The police, fire department and the gatdamn FBI?

LILLIE ANNE

Yes.

MARIE

Today? You gon do all that today?

LILLIE ANNE

Yes *TODAY*. She has to go TODAY! Or I'm going to take ACTION. That's what an intervention is gatdammit. You have to lay out the consequences of what will happen if she doesn't go to the rehab. *Today!*

MARIE

But damn you didn't tell us about all that earlier.

JAMES T

I thought you said this was suppose to be *voluntary*.

ADLEAN

You didn't say a damn thang about having to make threats.

LILLIE ANNE

IT'S A INTERVENTION!!

(Silence.)

JAMES T

So you're serious.

LILLIE ANNE

James T you gat a taser pulled out on a woman that's bound and gagged in a park and you asking me NOW if *I'm* serious.

JAMES T

Yes, are you seriously going to do all that if she don't go to Alaska?

LILLIE ANNE

. . . I'm serious.

MARIE

Wait a second, you can't call the police up in here right now.

LILLIE ANNE

Why the hell not?!

MARIE

What if *other people* besides Barbara might have some stuff on them that might be considered illegal or something?!! So we can't be callin the police up in here *today*!

(Lillie Anne steps as far away as she can . . .)

ADLEAN

(To Lillie Anne) Where the hell you going?

LILLIE ANNE

Can I speak to you all in private for a moment please?

JAMES T

We in an open-air park, how you gon speak in private?

LILLIE ANNE

Could you all come over here please so Barbara can't hear WHAT THE HELL I GAT TO SAY!!

(They start going over to her.)

THANK YOU!!!

(They are all near her now.)

(Whispering) Now the way an intervention works is you have to be willing to cut the person off from everyone they love so that they know you're serious.

ADLEAN

(Whispering) For how long?

LILLIE ANNE

(Whispering) What??

ADLEAN

(Whispering) For how long do we have to cut her off?

LILLIE ANNE

(Whispering) For forever if she don't get no help.

JAMES T

(Whispering) But what about if she goes to get help, knocks her counselor out with nunchucks, then climbs out a window and ends up back here.

LILLIE ANNE

(Whispering) . . . Then she is cut off!

MARIE

(Whispering) What if she *agrees*, to go get help, but she leaves without getting *all the way cured out* of being a crack head alcoholic ho, then do we still have to cut her off forever?

LILLIE ANNE

(Dumbfounded, whispering) She has to get off crack and stop drinking all together before she can come back into our lives. Period.

ADLEAN

(Whispering) But why is that?

LILLIE ANNE

(Whispering) Because you can't have *half* a gatdamn recovery from drugs and alcohol!!

MARIE

(Whispering) Why not?

LILLIE ANNE

(Whispering) Why not???

MARIE

(Whispering) Why the hell not? She don't get no credit for going *halfway*? I don't think that's right.

ADLEAN

(Whispering) I don't think that's right either.

I mean if Zippity Boom goes up there to Alaska and gets freezer burn or whatnot and has to come back here, how is that going to look that we just cut her the hell off.

JAMES T

(Whispering) You know what, they right. I'm starting to think Alaska might be too damn far. Ain't there other places closer to here that we could maybe send her. Like some place in the city. Maybe downtown.

LILLIE ANNE

(Whispering) NO!

JAMES T

(Whispering) Mama wouldn't like that we just up and sent her all the way—

LILLIE ANNE

(Whispering) Oh so *now* you worried about Mama!

ADLEAN

(Whispering) They gat to have some rehabs downtown somewhere, Lillie Anne.

(Beat.
    Adlean takes out her iPhone, pushes a button and speaks.)

(To iPhone, whispering) Siri, find a rehab near me.

SIRI VOICE

"I found twelve rehabilitation services . . . Eight of them are fairly close to you."

(Lillie Anne breaks the whispering.)

LILLIE ANNE

She goes to Alaska *tonight*!!

MARIE

Siri just found eight gatdamn rehabs right around the corner!

LILLIE ANNE

So what?

JAMES T

Why can't Zippity Boom just go to one of those?

LILLIE ANNE

Do you think you can just walk up into rehab and *check in*? It ain't a Ramada! Halcyon Dreams has the best quality care for someone in Barbara's position! I didn't just randomly pick Alaska! You are not suppose to send them to any place close. You want them *out* of their elements! You want them to have a completely new landscape and environment! They need to be close to nature and shit!

JAMES T

Will you listen to reason, Lillie Anne? Now we've done everything you said to do today. We came out here and pretended all this bullshit was a real barbecue and we spoke our gatdamn truths to Zippity Boom and the next thing is to get an answer out of her. Right? . . . *Is that right?*

LILLIE ANNE

Yes.

JAMES T

All we are asking is that you rethink for one second if she gotta go all the way out to east bum fuck Alaska. Is that *absolutely* necessary??

MARIE

Barbara might be better off in a rehab that wasn't three thousand some odd miles away from her gatdamn family.

ADLEAN

We know you feel like her being around glaciers and shit will help change her elements but there are four of us, if you count Zippity Boom, who think sending Barbara to Alaska is crazy!

(Silence.)

LILLIE ANNE

There are only a handful of us left. Therefore. This family, is a endangered species. And it's about time that we took a step in a different direction. If only for our own survival. We have already lost one brother and one sister to this shit and I be damned if I'm gonna sit up here and lose another one. I'll kill Zippity Boom myself if I have to but I ain't gon sit back anymore and just let this keep going on and on like it's the normal way of the gatdamn world. I been watching that damn show for going on five years now, as a matter of fact Barbara has sat up in my own house and watched that show with me and the crazy thing about it all is that, we like to act like it's just a gatdamn TV show. It *ain't*!

(Points to Barbara) It's right THERE in our face! Do you get it!! Do you see that it ain't a TV show! That it is right there in our *FACE*! Now I understand yall have reservations. I understand yall want Barbara to be safe and close to us but the entire

point of this is that she NOT be safe and close to us. The point is that she NOT be around any of the vices that have allowed her to easily access her drugs and alcohol. And I'm here to tell you that this entire family. Is a vice. This city. Is a vice. There-fore . . . *Alaska* . . . *Yoga* . . . And muthafuckin' *Horses*!!!

(Silence.)

ADLEAN

. . . And if she says no?

LILLIE ANNE

(Deadly) Then there will be gatdamn consequences.

ADLEAN

And that's the *crust* of the problem you are going to have with me.

MARIE

And me.

JAMES T

. . . And me.

(Silence.
Lillie Anne looks to them all. Then to Barbara. Then back to the others.)

LILLIE ANNE

What if she says yes.

JAMES T

She won't.

LILLIE ANNE

How bout we make a bet.

ADLEAN AND MARIE

A bet?

LILLIE ANNE

Yes. A bet. *(To Adlean)* You like to play them dime, quarter and dollar slots down on the boat, don'tcha. *(To James T)* You go to the race track every Saturday, Sunday, Monday, Tuesday and Wednesday, don'tcha. *(To Marie)* You play that funky monkey lucky spot scratch off every other hour *on* the hour like it's going out of style, don'tcha. *(To all)* So yall bettin folk. Right? Let's make a bet.

(Silence.)

JAMES T

Are we talkin real money?

ADLEAN

Or just some ole bullshit.

LILLIE ANNE

I'm talkin *real* money, honey. I'm talkin cold hard *cash.*

MARIE

Lillie Anne you know you don't gamble.

LILLIE ANNE

Git your money up.

ADLEAN

You know your gambling, is like your gatdamn dancin.

LILLIE ANNE

Answer the question. Do yall wanna bet?

(Silence.)

JAMES T

Put your money where your mouth at.

LILLIE ANNE

How much you gat?

MARIE

How much *you* gat?

ADLEAN

Yeah how much money *you* gat?

LILLIE ANNE

I gat more than ALL yall combined. And yall *know* this. So huddle up. And count your coins. Cuz I'm about to take all yall money *AND* send Zippity Boom to Alaska.

(Silence.

James T, Marie and Adlean race away and form a whispering huddle.

Lillie Anne retrieves the brochure and turns to Barbara.)

LILLIE ANNE

(Whisper) Look at all these pretty horses, Barbara. Look at all those sun salutations. Can't you just smell that clean air. They don't know that I know you useta love yoga and horses and shit . . . Now I know I'm not suppose to bribe you with money during an intervention. But that's exactly what the hell I'm doing. So I will pay you DOUBLE whatever they come up with . . . How about that?

(Silence.

Nothing from Barbara.

Lillie Anne and her other siblings come back together.

They look at each other for a moment.)

MARIE

We want your car.

ADLEAN

And your house.

JAMES T

That's our bet.

(Silence.)

LILLIE ANNE

Let me get this straight.

ADLEAN

Get it straight. Get. It. Straight.

LILLIE ANNE

If Barbara says no. Yall want my car.

MARIE

Yes.

LILLIE ANNE

And my house.

JAMES T

Yes.

(Silence.
Lillie Anne looks to Barbara and then back to others.
Silence.)

LILLIE ANNE

Okay.

JAMES T

Okay?

LILLIE ANNE

Okay.

ADLEAN AND MARIE

Okay??

LILLIE ANNE

Okay.

JAMES T

. . . Okay.

LILLIE ANNE

And if she says yes.
    Each one of you.
    Goes to rehab.

(Dead. Silence.)

. . . If Zippity Boom agrees to go to rehab. Then James T. All
that weed you smoke. Is done. Adlean. All them prescription
pills. Is done. Marie. All that recreational crack. Is done. The
Jack Daniels. Is done. The beers. Is done. The menthols. Is
done. The *gamblin*. Is *done*. Yall want my car. Yall want my
house . . . I want yall sobriety.

(Silence.)

JAMES T

Bet.

(Silence.)

ADLEAN

Bet.

(Marie looks to others like they've gone crazy.)

LILLIE ANNE

And you?

(Silence.)

MARIE

. . . Bet.

(Slowly. They all turn to Barbara. She looks to them.
Lillie Anne calmly walks over to Barbara. Lillie Anne carefully begins to ungag Barbara's mouth.
Silence. Then:)

LILLIE ANNE

Barbara, our sweet Zippity Boom, will you please take this offer to change your life, go to Halcyon Dreams Alcohol Rehab and Drug Addiction Treatment in Alaska, and become the person you were destined to be??

(Silence.
Barbara looks to her brother and sisters.
She opens her mouth to speak.)

BARBARA

AND.
CUT.

(Everyone drops character. The lights shift and the world is revealed to be completely Hollywood-soundstage fake. A white film crew, played by the white cast members, appears from various locations. However

elaborately or simply the production wishes, we are made aware that what we have been watching is the filming of one long set piece in a major motion picture.

    Soon the black actress playing Barbara speaks again.)

BARBARA

Alright everyone! Let's go again!

(Black.)

ACT TWO

BARBECUE

Projection: One Year Earlier.

White Barbara, fresh and modern, in a Middle America sort of way. She stands opposite Black Movie Star Barbara, who is chic, famous and fabulous in a Hollywood sort of way. She stands with an elegant gift box.

                    BLACK MOVIE STAR BARBARA
Hello.

(White Barbara stands in awed silence, struck dumb.
    This happens all the time to Black Movie Star Barbara so she lets White Barbara take her all in.
    Note: Every now and then, for no particular reason on earth, Black Movie Star Barbara will randomly speak passages of her dialogue with a British accent.)

(Smiles) . . . Yes it's really me . . . Hello.

WHITE BARBARA
(Awe) It's so great to meet you.

(They shake hands.)

BLACK MOVIE STAR BARBARA
(Famous modesty) It is an absolute honor and a pleasure.

WHITE BARBARA
No the pleasure is all—

BLACK MOVIE STAR BARBARA
I saw you on the phone as I was pulling up—

WHITE BARBARA
Damn.

BLACK MOVIE STAR BARBARA
(Calming) Noooo . . .

WHITE BARBARA
Shit.

BLACK MOVIE STAR BARBARA
Noooo.

WHITE BARBARA
Fuck.

BLACK MOVIE STAR BARBARA
Noooo.

WHITE BARBARA
Did I mess up somethin? Did I—

BLACK MOVIE STAR BARBARA
Absolutely not. Absolutely no. No. No. I'm. You know. The
paparazzi have been after me for months now after the whole—

WHITE BARBARA

I'm sorry.

BLACK MOVIE STAR BARBARA

No. It's not you. I'm just you know a little—I just wanted to ask you who you were talking to—

WHITE BARBARA

Nobody.

BLACK MOVIE STAR BARBARA

But you were talking—

WHITE BARBARA

No I wasn't.

BLACK MOVIE STAR BARBARA

I saw your mouth moving.

WHITE BARBARA

I was checking my—

BLACK MOVIE STAR BARBARA

I thought my assistant told you not to tell any—

WHITE BARBARA

I didn't.

BLACK MOVIE STAR BARBARA

I thought we made it clear that I only wanted to meet with you—and *only* you—at *this* moment in our—

WHITE BARBARA

I was checking my messages.

(Silence.)

I was speaking to my sponsor.

BLACK MOVIE STAR BARBARA

. . .

WHITE BARBARA

She won't be a problem. I promise. I was told you were going to be here a half hour ago. So I—she called. And I just you know . . .

BLACK MOVIE STAR BARBARA

Just as long as she knows—

WHITE BARBARA

Absolutely. She would never. It's fine.

BLACK MOVIE STAR BARBARA

It's fine?

WHITE BARBARA

It's absolutely fine. She's my sponsor. So you know. Everything is . . . private . . . confi . . . dential.

(Silence.)

BLACK MOVIE STAR BARBARA

I wanted to be in the zone for a moment. You know. *Your zone.* Be in the real space be in the zone be with you and it's not often that I can do this without you know—

WHITE BARBARA

I know. I completely get—

BLACK MOVIE STAR BARBARA

I have less than a hour to sort of . . . you know—soak up.

WHITE BARBARA

Yes.

BLACK MOVIE STAR BARBARA

The environs.

WHITE BARBARA

I completely get it—

BLACK MOVIE STAR BARBARA

And that's more than most—I'm just saying this is a *big deal* that I'm here . . . doing this . . . with you.

WHITE BARBARA

I'm *truly* sorry.

(Silence.)

BLACK MOVIE STAR BARBARA

Alright.

WHITE BARBARA

Alright.

BLACK MOVIE STAR BARBARA

Alright.

(Silence. They look to each other.)

It's going to be a great movie . . . And I'm not just saying that because I'm writing, directing, producing, starring, and sangin the title song. I really think it's going to be a contender for the Big One. Best Picture. I mean the scene of your intervention in this park . . . Awards. Buckets. Of. Awards . . . Half-dozen naked golden men in my arms—

WHITE BARBARA

It was a conference call . . . I was . . . on a . . . uh . . . I was on a conference call when you pulled up . . . It's . . . it was a group . . . sort of a . . . yeah . . . NA has this group that . . . uh you can . . . conference . . . call . . . session . . .

(Silence.)

> BLACK MOVIE STAR BARBARA

So everyone in your . . . *group* . . . knows I'm here.

> WHITE BARBARA

Everyone? . . . Uh . . . Yes.

(Black Movie Star Barbara sighs.
  Silence.
  She takes out her cell phone, dials, and eventually speaks.)

> BLACK MOVIE STAR BARBARA

(Into cell phone) Could you have security park the decoy in front of the Western Gate and don't let anyone in . . . thank you . . . *(She sighs)* Yes. Yes. No one. Period.

(She hangs up.)

> WHITE BARBARA

Wow. You can do that?

> BLACK MOVIE STAR BARBARA

Do what? Speak on a phone?

> WHITE BARBARA

. . . Close down a park? A public park.

> BLACK MOVIE STAR BARBARA

(Honest) . . . Do you know who I am?

> WHITE BARBARA

Yes. I think I know.

> BLACK MOVIE STAR BARBARA

Then you should know that I can close down a public park.

> WHITE BARBARA

Wow . . . Well . . . I didn't know that.

(Silence.)

BLACK MOVIE STAR BARBARA

Alright. Now—

(White Barbara's cell phone rings.
Black Movie Star Barbara stares at White Barbara.
The cell phone continues to ring.
White Barbara motions to answer it.
Black Movie Star Barbara calmly shakes her head for her NOT
to answer the phone.
They wait for it to stop ringing.
Finally. Silence.
Black Movie Star Barbara begins to speak.)

Alright. Now—

(A strange beep comes from White Barbara's cell phone.)

WHITE BARBARA

. . . Voice mail.

(Another strange beep from the cell phone.)

. . . Text.

(A final strange beep.)

. . . Tweet.

BLACK MOVIE STAR BARBARA

Can I have your phone?

WHITE BARBARA

. . .

> BLACK MOVIE STAR BARBARA

Just for the length of my stay.

> WHITE BARBARA

I'll turn it off—

> BLACK MOVIE STAR BARBARA

Well—

> WHITE BARBARA

I'll turn it completely—

> BLACK MOVIE STAR BARBARA

I'm gonna need your phone.

(Silence.
   White Barbara eventually gives up her phone.)

And . . . Could you walk off in that direction?

(She points and White Barbara looks off.)

> WHITE BARBARA

. . . For what?

> BLACK MOVIE STAR BARBARA

I would actually like to begin by communing with the space . . .
alone . . . and then I'll invite you in.

> WHITE BARBARA

. . . Invite me in? It's a public . . . park.

> BLACK MOVIE STAR BARBARA

Could you just walk off in that direction.

> WHITE BARBARA

. . . How far in that direction?

BLACK MOVIE STAR BARBARA

I'll tell you when to stop.

(Silence.
Eventually, White Barbara slowly walks offstage.)

. . . Uh . . . keep going.

(Silence.)

WHITE BARBARA

(From off) . . . Here?

BLACK MOVIE STAR BARBARA

. . . Further!

(Silence.
Then, once White Barbara has reached as far offstage as humanly possible, she speaks again.)

WHITE BARBARA

(From further off) . . . Here?

BLACK MOVIE STAR BARBARA

Perfect.

(Black Movie Star Barbara looks around the park as if she's never seen one before.
She breathes in fresh clean air . . .
She communes with the space.
Soon she motions for White Barbara, who eventually reenters.)

I'll need you to be absolutely honest with me and not let me get away with anything from my ole bag of tricks.

WHITE BARBARA

Um . . . I didn't know you had a . . . bag of . . . tricks . . . but . . . Okay.

BLACK MOVIE STAR BARBARA

If I'm going to inhabit this world of yours then I need *YOU* to *keep me in it.*

WHITE BARBARA

. . . Sure.

BLACK MOVIE STAR BARBARA

I want my *struggle* to be *real* and—

WHITE BARBARA

Didn't you grow up in the Marcy Projects in Brooklyn?

(Silence.)

BLACK MOVIE STAR BARBARA

I beg your pardon?

WHITE BARBARA

. . . I thought I read in some magazine about you growing up in—

BLACK MOVIE STAR BARBARA

You read something wrong in some magazine. I don't know nuthin bout no projects in Brooklyn.

(Silence.)

You must be thinkin bout some Jay Z song or somethin . . .

WHITE BARBARA

. . . Yeah.

BLACK MOVIE STAR BARBARA

. . . Yeah.

WHITE BARBARA

. . . Okay.

BLACK MOVIE STAR BARBARA

. . . Okay.

(Silence.)

We should film it right here. Shoot the *entire* movie. *In this city*. Around this very park. Right here. And not dress it up. No backlot. Soundstage . . . But *here*. Right here. *(Relish)* It *smells* like barbecue. *(She breathes deeply)* It reeks of the truth, doesn't it? This place is *authentic*.

WHITE BARBARA

. . . Well people do actually barbecue here.

BLACK MOVIE STAR BARBARA

And I want *real people* . . . *real folk* . . . *real talk* . . . You know what I mean?

WHITE BARBARA

I think so. Real talk.

BLACK MOVIE STAR BARBARA

I don't want a bunch of glamour pusses . . . I might just cast it with *nobodies*.

WHITE BARBARA

Nobodies.

BLACK MOVIE STAR BARBARA

Un-heard-ofs.

WHITE BARBARA

. . . Okay.

> ### BLACK MOVIE STAR BARBARA
>
> Just go out into the streets, into the *COMMUNITY*, you know, or better yet into Popeyes Chicken and Waffles and grab some *real folk*.

> ### WHITE BARBARA
>
> . . . I see.

> ### BLACK MOVIE STAR BARBARA
>
> We don't need a bunch of airbrushed faces "*pretendin.*"

> ### WHITE BARBARA
>
> I was wondering—

> ### BLACK MOVIE STAR BARBARA
>
> And I want you on the set with us . . .

> ### WHITE BARBARA
>
> Me?

> ### BLACK MOVIE STAR BARBARA
>
> *Every. Day.*

> ### WHITE BARBARA
>
> Every day.

> ### BLACK MOVIE STAR BARBARA
>
> Yes! Making sure we *maintain* the *truth* . . .

> ### WHITE BARBARA
>
> I would . . . love that, I'm sure— Could I ask you something—

> ### BLACK MOVIE STAR BARBARA
>
> How were you tied?

> ### WHITE BARBARA
>
> Sorry?

BLACK MOVIE STAR BARBARA

How were you tied up?

WHITE BARBARA

Um . . .

BLACK MOVIE STAR BARBARA

Show me.

WHITE BARBARA

I don't . . . really remember. That was over a year or so ago—

BLACK MOVIE STAR BARBARA

(Sexual) . . . Show me.

(White Barbara looks at her.
Black Movie Star Barbara smiles.
. . . White Barbara awkwardly approximates how she was tied
up . . .
Black Movie Star Barbara studies White Barbara who holds in
position, awkwardly.
Then:)

I don't believe it.

WHITE BARBARA

Believe what?

BLACK MOVIE STAR BARBARA

I don't believe it happened that way.

WHITE BARBARA

What way?

BLACK MOVIE STAR BARBARA

That way.

WHITE BARBARA
Well it did.

BLACK MOVIE STAR BARBARA
It's just not believable.

WHITE BARBARA
(Removing herself from pillar) I'm sorry if my life isn't believable—

BLACK MOVIE STAR BARBARA
Oh, I believe *you*.

WHITE BARBARA
But you just said—

BLACK MOVIE STAR BARBARA
I just don't believe *it*.

WHITE BARBARA
What???

BLACK MOVIE STAR BARBARA
And I don't believe anybody else will.

WHITE BARBARA
If we're talking about believability—first off *you're* black.

(Silence.
  Silence.
  Silence.
  *Black Movie Star Barbara moves close to White Barbara and the
following conversation is whispered.)*

BLACK MOVIE STAR BARBARA
You are sure you know who you're talking to, right?

WHITE BARBARA

(Looking around) . . . You?

BLACK MOVIE STAR BARBARA

Yes . . . Moi.

WHITE BARBARA

You're black.

BLACK MOVIE STAR BARBARA

I'm not black.

WHITE BARBARA

You're not black?

BLACK MOVIE STAR BARBARA

I'm a movie star . . . And a sanga.

WHITE BARBARA

Yeah you're a black movie star singer.

BLACK MOVIE STAR BARBARA

No, my dear. I'm a *Movie. Star. Sanga.*

WHITE BARBARA

Okay. But. You. Are. Black.

BLACK MOVIE STAR BARBARA

I don't think you are understanding me. You see. When you reach the level of fame that I have. Race. Sorta. Falls away.

WHITE BARBARA

Falls away.

BLACK MOVIE STAR BARBARA

Falls away. Like over a cliff. When you are as famous as I am, race, takes a running nosedive over a cliff and you are just left with . . . Movie Star Sanga.

(Silence.)

WHITE BARBARA

. . . Okay.

BLACK MOVIE STAR BARBARA

So . . . if we could leave race. Like completely out of the conversation. Like way out. Of the conversation. Like all the way back in Africa out of the conversation. That would be great.

WHITE BARBARA

. . . Okay.

BLACK MOVIE STAR BARBARA

And I think you should apologize.

WHITE BARBARA

For what?

BLACK MOVIE STAR BARBARA

Well, I think you know for what.

WHITE BARBARA

Look—

BLACK MOVIE STAR BARBARA

One. Million. Dollars. Is what they are planning on paying you. For your *rights*. To your *life*. So I think you will indeed apologize to the Movie Star Sanga that you just insulted by calling her *(Mouths) black.*

(Black Movie Star Barbara steps away to where she was before. White Barbara looks at her for a moment.

She looks around to see if this is some hidden camera joke and realizes that it isn't.

No longer whispering:)

WHITE BARBARA

. . . I'm sorry . . . for calling you black.

BLACK MOVIE STAR BARBARA

Apology accepted.

WHITE BARBARA

Thank you . . .

BLACK MOVIE STAR BARBARA

My schedule is extremely tight.

WHITE BARBARA

. . . Yes.

BLACK MOVIE STAR BARBARA

So.

WHITE BARBARA

So.

BLACK MOVIE STAR BARBARA

Sooo.

WHITE BARBARA

Where would you like to begin—

BLACK MOVIE STAR BARBARA

When was the last time you smoked crack?

(Beat.)

WHITE BARBARA

I never smoked . . . crack, I smoked meth.

BLACK MOVIE STAR BARBARA

Oh, we have to change that to crack for the movie.

> WHITE BARBARA

But that's not—

> BLACK MOVIE STAR BARBARA

You have to be a crackhead. Black folks don't smoke meth.

> WHITE BARBARA

Uh . . . Well actually . . .

> BLACK MOVIE STAR BARBARA

Black folks in movies don't smoke meth. Black folks in movies smoke weed. And crack.

> WHITE BARBARA

. . . Okay.

> BLACK MOVIE STAR BARBARA

So . . . when was the last time you smoked crack?

(Beat.)

> WHITE BARBARA

As I wrote in my memoir, there were a couple of relapses but for the most part I don't happen to smoke "crack" anymore.

> BLACK MOVIE STAR BARBARA

"For the most part."

> WHITE BARBARA

For the most part, yes.

> BLACK MOVIE STAR BARBARA

Why is that?

> WHITE BARBARA

Well, because "crack" is highly addictive.

BLACK MOVIE STAR BARBARA

And?

WHITE BARBARA

And I usually sell all my shit and run around half naked when I'm on it.

BLACK MOVIE STAR BARBARA

. . . That never stopped you before.

WHITE BARBARA

I know.

BLACK MOVIE STAR BARBARA

What exactly is stopping you now?

WHITE BARBARA

. . . Well in my memoirs I write about—

BLACK MOVIE STAR BARBARA

Fuck your memoirs.

WHITE BARBARA

Fuck my memoirs?

BLACK MOVIE STAR BARBARA

Fuck your memoirs. I have to embody THE TRUTH of the character and not simply what you put in some book.

WHITE BARBARA

It's not "some" book. It's my life story.

BLACK MOVIE STAR BARBARA

I'm more interested in what's *not* in your "life story."

WHITE BARBARA

But you're buying the rights to my memoirs.

BLACK MOVIE STAR BARBARA

I don't buy rights, darling.

WHITE BARBARA

Then who does?

BLACK MOVIE STAR BARBARA

The studio is *considering* buying your *life* rights.

WHITE BARBARA

Considering . . . Oh . . .

BLACK MOVIE STAR BARBARA

And the studio has flown me here on the company jet in order
for *you* to convince *me* that I should star in this movie as *you*. A
crackhead alcoholic ho.

(Silence.)

You thought I had already signed on?

WHITE BARBARA

. . . Yes.

BLACK MOVIE STAR BARBARA

I have not signed on. The studio is hoping this visit—

WHITE BARBARA

My literary agent said you were practically signed, sealed and
delivered?

BLACK MOVIE STAR BARBARA

What am I, a letter?

WHITE BARBARA

. . . My literary agent—

BLACK MOVIE STAR BARBARA

She lied.

WHITE BARBARA

But—

BLACK MOVIE STAR BARBARA

They all lie. We're in the business of lying.

(Silence.)

WHITE BARBARA

Um . . . I actually . . . never was a whore.

BLACK MOVIE STAR BARBARA

Who said you were a whore?

WHITE BARBARA

You did.

BLACK MOVIE STAR BARBARA

No I didn't.

WHITE BARBARA

You said I was suppose to convince you to play me, a crackhead alcoholic whore.

BLACK MOVIE STAR BARBARA

No. I said a crackhead alcoholic *ho*. Not a whore. A *ho*.

WHITE BARBARA

Well I never was a whore. Or a ho.

BLACK MOVIE STAR BARBARA

How is anybody suppose to believe you're a crackhead. *And* an alcoholic. *And* you *ain't* a ho? . . . com'on now that don't make sense.

WHITE BARBARA

I don't know but . . . I'm sorry. I was never a ho.

(Silence.)

BLACK MOVIE STAR BARBARA

You smell like a drink, you know that?

WHITE BARBARA

What?

BLACK MOVIE STAR BARBARA

You smell like you put yourself together this morning and had yourself a nice little drink to rub out the edges and afterwards you gargled for thirty minutes with something awful and peppermint flavored, am I right?

WHITE BARBARA

(She's right) Wait a minute.

BLACK MOVIE STAR BARBARA

Look. I'm going to do this stupid movie about your stupid little life. And the reason why I'm going to do this stupid movie about your stupid little life is because I want some *Oscars* . . . Just like anybody else . . . Simple as that . . . Folks like to think of me as just some Sanga who became a Movie Star. But I'm not just some damn Sanga who became a Movie Star. Them dummies at that studio keep after me about when I'm gonna start recording the soundtrack. That's all they care about "when is the soundtrack coming out." We don't even have a damn script and they asking about a soundtrack!! I'm not just some damn Sanga!! Who became a Movie Star. You know how many units I sold off my last soundtrack—

WHITE BARBARA

No.

BLACK MOVIE STAR BARBARA

Ten million . . . ten gatdamn million soundtracks sold!! That's the *only* reason they are even *considering* letting me do this damn stupid movie about your stupid little life. But I'm gonna fool *all* of em. I still got me some tricks up my sleeves. I'm gonna win me some bald-headed butt-naked golden muthafuckas. You feel me???

(Silence.)

. . . You one em fake bitches?

WHITE BARBARA

Excuse me?!!

BLACK MOVIE STAR BARBARA

(Ghetto) You one em fake alcoholic crackhead bitch ass *hos?*

(Dead. Silence.)

WHITE BARBARA

You know what, I've stood here for the last several minutes as you rattled on and on about whatever crazy shit you were rattling on and on about—telling me I'm not believable, you're not black and I'm a crackhead alcoholic *ho* . . . Well Ms. MOVIE STAR SANGA, *MY LIFE* is believable!!! Because it's true. It's *YOUR LIFE* that ain't believable. You come here like a fairy tale in your *company jet* with your "walk over there" so you can *commune* get into your *zone* for some awards—you want *real talk* . . . here's some *real talk* . . . *Fuck you bitch!!*

(White Barbara starts leave.)

BLACK MOVIE STAR BARBARA

That's it!! That's her! That's *Zippity Boom.* That's! Who I came down here to speak to—that's who I wanna portray. *NOW.* We are *READY*!!! Ready for some serious chitchat. I need to get down to the nitty-gritty. I want you to talk to me just like that . . . like you use to talk before rehab. Okay? Let's have some Zippity Boom-Boom!!

(White Barbara just looks at her.)

. . . Somethin wrong?
     So look. I guess you've heard about my little incident?

WHITE BARBARA

You mean the one where you flipped your—

BLACK MOVIE STAR BARBARA

Yeah. That one.

WHITE BARBARA

Yes I heard.

BLACK MOVIE STAR BARBARA

I just left rehab.

WHITE BARBARA

Rehab rehab? Or just rehab.

BLACK MOVIE STAR BARBARA

Rehab rehab.

WHITE BARBARA

. . .

BLACK MOVIE STAR BARBARA

We've kept it very hush-hush.

WHITE BARBARA

. . .

BLACK MOVIE STAR BARBARA

So while I'm sitting up in rehab with all this time to kill . . .
I had all these scripts being sent to me that needed a title song
to the soundtrack and I just kept reading *this* load of crap and
reading *that* load of crap and then they sent me the galleys
to your memoirs and I was like, Wow, this is a memoir about
rehab and I'm sitting up here in *rehab* . . .

(Honest) . . . You know, the people I use to trust . . . before
the money . . . before the fame . . . they all let me down . . . they
didn't care about me . . . they just cared about *The Voice* . . . so in
rehab . . . I had to come to grips with that . . . like in your book
. . . when your sister says that she comes to you with "truth and
love" . . . I had to learn that in order for me to love myself . . .
I had to accept the truth . . . So when the studio sent me your
galleys and asked if I could sing a song for its soundtrack when
it was made into a movie . . . I wrote them back and told them
that I wanted to make it MY DAMN SELF . . . I wanted to
star, write, direct, produce and *THEN* I'd sang on the damn
soundtrack. So they sent me here . . . That's what selling ten
million records off a soundtrack can get you. Opportunity . . .
(To herself) Even if it don't come with a damn bit of respect.

(Beat.)

(Close) You got anything?

WHITE BARBARA

Excuse me?

BLACK MOVIE STAR BARBARA

(Closer) You holding anything? . . . A little bump, maybe?

WHITE BARBARA

. . . No. I'm clean.

(Silence.)

(Serious) . . . I'm clean . . . And I don't do "crack."

BLACK MOVIE STAR BARBARA

(Offended) I don't do crack either. I make too much money to do crack.

WHITE BARBARA

. . . Good.

BLACK MOVIE STAR BARBARA

. . . Good.

(Silence.)

WHITE BARBARA

I've heard that before.

BLACK MOVIE STAR BARBARA

Heard what before?

WHITE BARBARA

"I make too much money to do crack."

BLACK MOVIE STAR BARBARA

Yeah, you heard it because I just said it.

WHITE BARBARA

No. *Before* you said it, I heard it. *Before.*

BLACK MOVIE STAR BARBARA

. . . Well you should go get that checked out.

(Silence.)

Look. We got off to a shaky start. Let's make like I just got here . . . reset the clock . . . begin again . . . like none of this ever—

WHITE BARBARA

Are you a lesbian?

(Silence.)

Real talk . . .

(Silence.)

I read in a magazine—there have been rumors since the time you lived in the Marcy Projects about you being—

BLACK MOVIE STAR BARBARA

I grew up in the church. I'm married. With a child.

(Silence.)

WHITE BARBARA

. . . Are you a lesbian—?

BLACK MOVIE STAR BARBARA

—I learned to sing. In the church . . . I love my husband and my—

WHITE BARBARA

(Honest) It's all lies.

. . . My memoirs. It's all lies. From start to finish. You're right. It's not believable. I made it all up. In rehab . . . In rehab I read this one memoir that everybody told me had sold the most around the world . . . And I read it . . . the *strength* I got just from reading this one little book . . . this memoir . . . and then one day . . . another woman came into rehab . . . and she was . . . she was in the bottoms . . . *deep* in the *rock bottoms*—I went to my room and got this memoir and I handed it to her . . . because you see someone had handed it to me in my rock bottoms and it had changed my life . . . I handed it to *her* . . .

and you know what she did . . . she slapped it out of my hand
. . . "That's som ole bullshit" . . . "Ain't you heard" . . . "That's
som ole bullshit" . . . I picked it up off the floor and right there
. . . right in the front of the book . . . in the part where nobody
reads where nobody looks at— *"This book . . . is a combination of
facts . . . and certain embellishments . . . Names, dates, places, events
and details . . . have been changed, invented and altered . . . for literary effect. The reader should not consider this book anything other
than a work of literature."* I remember like it was yesterday . . .
you'd think my heart would sink . . . that I'd be upset . . . angry
. . . you'd think I'd want to find this man who changed my state
of being . . . who gave me hope against all hope . . . you'd think
I want to find him and *spit* in his face . . . but instead I thought
. . . Wait a minute . . . Hell, I know how to lie . . . I know
how to *invent* shit *alter* details I'm a gatdamn expert at *changing*
the truth . . . I've been doing that my whole damn life . . . So
I started writing—

BLACK MOVIE STAR BARBARA

It's a lie?

WHITE BARBARA

My life. It's not believable because it's all lies.

BLACK MOVIE STAR BARBARA

(Whispering) All of it? . . . It's all—

WHITE BARBARA

(Whispering) Are you a lesbian . . . A rug muncher. A clam licker.
A muff diver. A tit gobbler. A bumper to bumper.

(A very long silence.
  Black Movie Star Barbara suffers.)

. . . What's her name? . . . Uhhh . . . uhhh . . . Tina . . . right . . . Tina?? . . . I read about her . . . *(Beat)* You know, I had a sister named Tina . . . *(Beat)* And I uh . . . I say her name sometimes and . . . It sorta attaches itself . . . she had uh . . . she had three beautiful girls . . . and she— . . . she couldn't cope . . . I watched her . . . we all did . . . You couldn't say nuthin to her . . . you couldn't do nuthin for her . . . she walked around for years looking like she was eight months pregnant . . . bloated . . . hairless . . . her skin was all . . . and still . . . I stepped right into her shoes . . . started even before she was gone and I was much worse . . . the shit I did . . . the stuff I got into out there running the street . . . was much worse . . . but uh . . . every now and then . . . in the middle of the . . . the mess of my life . . . I would remember . . . that I had a sister . . . named Tina . . . *(Beat)* Your Tina, she was your one true thing, wasn't she?

BLACK MOVIE STAR BARBARA
What the hell makes you say that?

WHITE BARBARA
. . . You flipped your car . . .

(A long silence.)

BLACK MOVIE STAR BARBARA
(Resentful/mocking) My Tina . . . She wanted us to stand out in the light . . . let it shine on the both of us . . . said it was easy these days . . .

Find a talk show and just . . . you know . . . make an event of it all . . . said . . . we should put all the rumors to rest . . . "Tell the world who you are" . . . Who I am??? — . . . I'm a *Movie Star Sanga* . . . and that's all that spotlight can hold . . . So I had to let her go . . . Went to her . . . Told her I had to let her go . . . and I . . .

(Long unnatural silence.)

I flipped my car . . . thought that would end it . . . but they found me and brought me back . . . they always find me . . . and bring me back . . .

(Silence.)

> WHITE BARBARA

. . . You regret it? . . . Any of it? . . .

> BLACK MOVIE STAR BARBARA

Money makes it so I don't have to regret . . .

> WHITE BARBARA

Just wondering if folks who have everything—

> BLACK MOVIE STAR BARBARA

(Too strong) I don't have *everything*.

(Silence.)

> WHITE BARBARA

You're addicted to her.

(Silence.)

> BLACK MOVIE STAR BARBARA

. . . I have a bad habit . . .

> WHITE BARBARA

I bet you do . . .

> BLACK MOVIE STAR BARBARA

Just like you . . .

> WHITE BARBARA

Just like me.

(Silence.)

BLACK MOVIE STAR BARBARA
And you're a liar.

WHITE BARBARA
. . . That I am.

BLACK MOVIE STAR BARBARA
Well this is going to be an interesting partnership.

WHITE BARBARA
What?

BLACK MOVIE STAR BARBARA
Our movie. You and I.

(Silence.)

Junkie to junkie.

WHITE BARBARA
You still wanna do the movie?

BLACK MOVIE STAR BARBARA
Of course I'm gonna do the movie.

WHITE BARBARA
Even though you know I made it all up?

BLACK MOVIE STAR BARBARA
You don't get it do you darling . . . *We all make it all up.*

(Silence.)

Don't you see how perfect this is . . . Don't you see the symmetry. The hook. In rehab . . . You came up with a bunch of lies. In rehab . . . I read your bunch of lies . . . And we're gonna take that bunch of lies . . . all the way to the muthafuckin Oscars.

(Long silence.)

WHITE BARBARA

(Awe) Wow . . . You're good.

BLACK MOVIE STAR BARBARA

Tell me something I don't know.

WHITE BARBARA

(Awe) You're really fucking good. Here I am . . . terrified since the start that someone would find out it was all lies . . . and here you are . . . Happy to know it's all bullshit. Everything is bullshit.

BLACK MOVIE STAR BARBARA

Everythang. Is bullshit.

(Silence.)

(Relish) Can you smell it?

WHITE BARBARA

(Relish) I can smell it.

BLACK MOVIE STAR BARBARA

Yasss . . . My transformation during the middle part of the film, will secure me various nominations. *(Ghetto)* But only if I'm "toe-up from the flo-up" in the first third.

WHITE BARBARA

Wait.

BLACK MOVIE STAR BARBARA

What?

WHITE BARBARA

What are these voices you keep putting on?

BLACK MOVIE STAR BARBARA

What voices? You hearing voices?

WHITE BARBARA

That ghetto-British-voice-thing you've been doing.

BLACK MOVIE STAR BARBARA

(Deadly serious) I have no idea what you're talking about. And I don't have a lot of time. I have to get back to the center before—

WHITE BARBARA

You're *still* in rehab?

BLACK MOVIE STAR BARBARA

I told you I just left there.

WHITE BARBARA

And you're going back now?

BLACK MOVIE STAR BARBARA

The studio negotiated to get me out for a few hours today.

WHITE BARBARA

You don't look like you just left rehab today.

BLACK MOVIE STAR BARBARA

The studio sent a makeup and costume crew with the company jet.

WHITE BARBARA

Wow.

                    BLACK MOVIE STAR BARBARA
Now let's get down to the—

                    WHITE BARBARA
(Fierce) When do I get to ride in the company jet?

(Silence.)

                    BLACK MOVIE STAR BARBARA
What makes you think that you would get to ride in the
company jet?

                    WHITE BARBARA
The same thing that makes you think that you would get some
Oscars.

(Silence.)

My *rights*. To my *life*.

(Silence.)

                    BLACK MOVIE STAR BARBARA
. . . I see.

                    WHITE BARBARA
And I want. Three.

                    BLACK MOVIE STAR BARBARA
Three what?

                    WHITE BARBARA
Three million.

(Silence.)

BLACK MOVIE STAR BARBARA

You want the studio to pay you three million dollars—

WHITE BARBARA

I want *you* to get the studio to pay me *three million dollars.*

BLACK MOVIE STAR BARBARA

Are you high? They ain't gonna pay you no damn three million dollars.

WHITE BARBARA

Then fuck you. And fuck the studio.

BLACK MOVIE STAR BARBARA

Fuck me and fuck the studio?

WHITE BARBARA

Yes. You said it. Fuck my memoirs. Fuck you. And fuck the studio.

BLACK MOVIE STAR BARBARA

You're ready to throw this all away?

WHITE BARBARA

"You don't get it do you darling . . ." *We have already thrown this all away.*

(Silence.)

Don't you see how perfect this is . . . Don't you see the symmetry. The hook. In rehab . . .

You read a story that will get you a bunch of Oscars. In rehab . . . I wrote that story, that gets you your bunch of Oscars . . . And we're gonna take that bunch of Oscars . . . all the way to the muthafuckin bank.

(Silence.)

                    BLACK MOVIE STAR BARBARA
Wow . . . you're good.

                          WHITE BARBARA
Tell me something I don't know.

                    BLACK MOVIE STAR BARBARA
. . . Can I see Zippity Boom now?

                          WHITE BARBARA
What?

                    BLACK MOVIE STAR BARBARA
I'd like to talk to Zippity Boom now.

(Black Movie Star Barbara starts to unwrap the gift box.)

                          WHITE BARBARA
That was just a—a nickname that my family use to call me when
I was in a really bad way. It's not like I can just become Zippity
Boom— I mean I'd have to—

*(Black Movie Star Barbara has opened the elegant gift box and
reveals that inside is a ziplock baggie filled with a lighter, a crack pipe
and rocks of crack cocaine.*
    White Barbara jumps and moves far away.)

(Serious) What the fuck is that?

                    BLACK MOVIE STAR BARBARA
Motivation.

                          WHITE BARBARA
(Terrified) . . . I can't do this.

BLACK MOVIE STAR BARBARA

Sure you can. Don't worry I won't tell.

(White Barbara begins to involuntarily move toward the drugs.)

WHITE BARBARA

If anybody found out about this . . .

BLACK MOVIE STAR BARBARA

I've closed down the entire park, Barbara.

WHITE BARBARA

(Closer. Secret) . . . People will find out . . .

BLACK MOVIE STAR BARBARA

The studio is buying the rights to your life story. Remember. Not to the truth . . . I just need to commune a little with the protagonist.

(White Barbara touches the crack-filled ziplock.
    She unzips the ziplock baggie.
    She hands the lighter to Black Movie Star Barbara who lights the crack pipe.
    The two women do a hit.)

(Dark) Zippity.

WHITE BARBARA

(Dark) Boom.

(Black.)

BLACKOUT

Present day.
   The white cast is back and frozen in place.
   James T with a beer to his lips.
   Marie with a bottle of Jack Daniels to her lips.
   Adlean with a cigarette to her lips.
   And Lillie Anne with her cell phone in hand, mid-text.
   Barbara stands in front of them. Frozen.
   Then:

                    LILLIE ANNE
You wrote a book?

                    BARBARA
Yes. A memoir.

                    MARIE
What the hell is a "memoir."

BARBARA

My life story.

ADLEAN

And you put us in it.

BARBARA

You're part of my life.

JAMES T

And somebody published *that*?

BARBARA

I found a great literary agent.

MARIE

What the hell do you know about great literary Asians?

LILLIE ANNE

An agent. Not an Asian. Fool.

MARIE

Oh.

ADLEAN

I still don't understand what the hell this got to do with us.

BARBARA

There's a movie that's been made.

JAMES T

A movie about what?

BARBARA

Us.

ADLEAN

How much did they pay you for this gatdamn movie about *us*?

BARBARA

(Lie) . . . One million dollars.

(Silence.)

JAMES T

(Dead serious) Bitch, are you back on crack?

BARBARA

. . . No.

LILLIE ANNE

One million dollars.

BARBARA

One million. Dollars.

LILLIE ANNE

Let me understand somethin, are you standin up here tellin us that we rich . . . ?

BARBARA

Yes.

(Silence.
    James T, Marie, Adlean and Lillie Anne look to Barbara as if she has lost her mind. Again.
    Then. Barbara smiles.)

BARBARA

WE ARE RICH, BITCHES!!!

(JOY ERUPTS!!

They all jump around like complete fools having won the lottery.

Soon, because of their age and "bad habits," they all have to catch their breath. Bent over and holding onto each other, they speak between ecstatic gasps.)

MARIE

We gonna be famous!

ADLEAN

(Gasps) I can't believe it. I just can't believe it, Zippity Boom you came through. Finally. You came through.

JAMES T

(Gasps) Who would have thought you'd do something like this with your life. From the crackhead whore you started out as.

BARBARA

Well that's the thing. I changed the crack into meth.

MARIE

(Serious) I didn't know you could change crack into meth.

(Beat.)

BARBARA

In my memoirs. I changed the crack into meth.

ADLEAN

Who playing me?

BARBARA

Well, that's the other interesting part . . . that's why I called you all out here today . . . First off. I'm gonna need you all . . . to go to rehab . . . for three months.

(More silence.

Then Adlean, Marie, Lillie Anne and James T break out into laughter.

They continue laughing until they realize that Barbara is not laughing.

Silence.)

(All business) I wrote a letter that I want to read to you all . . .

(She takes out the letter.)

(Reading) "Marie, Adlean, Lillie Anne and James T.

I have made up almost the entirety of my memoirs with lies, out of which they have made a film, titled *Barbecue*. I wrote that you all brought me to this park and performed a barbecue intervention on me. That you all tased me with a taser and tied and gagged me. James T, I gave you a pot habit. Marie, I gave you a minor crack habit. Adlean, I gave you cancer. And Lillian Anne, I made you into a stuck-up bitch. But most importantly, I wrote, in my memoirs, that in order to get me to go to rehab, you all also agreed to go to rehab. Reporters are going to be asking each of you about your rehabilitation. Therefore, I have researched and I am providing four well-established rehabilitation centers across the country that are prepared to admit each of you today, for the duration of no less than ninety days. So Marie, Adlean, Lillie Anne and James T, if you want your fucking *two hundred thousand* dollars. You all have to take your asses to rehab, today."

(Dead silence.

She gently folds the letter up and puts it away.)

(Zippity Boom) And if you do not take this gift of *new hope* that I am providing you and go to rehab . . . I am prepared to make your lives, a living hell. *Again.* If you thought I was a wreck,

before my rehab. Wait until you see my next relapse. If you each and every one of you, do not take this gift of *new life* that I am presenting to you. I will tell the world that our parents beat us. And that you each molested me. And that you tried to sell me, into white slavery. And the world will believe me. Just like they believe my memoir.

(Silence.)

Alright. Are there any questions?

(Silence.

Then James T, Marie, Adlean and Lillie Anne all raise their hands, still looking at Barbara like she's crazy.)

James T?

JAMES T
(Serious) Who the fuck are you?

BARBARA
. . . I'm Zippity Boom, I'm the one that if you listen to me carefully and do as I say, will make you rich and famous.

(Lillie Anne's hand goes back up.)

Lillie Anne?

LILLIE ANNE
I'm supposed to go to rehab just for being a stuck-up bitch?

BARBARA
As a matter of fact. Yes. You see, what was revealed in the test screening of the movie, was that your character has control issues. And the test audience felt like you should go to rehab to

deal with that. So the director brought the cast back for reshoots. And now your character goes to rehab with the rest of us.

LILLIE ANNE

Well . . . Unlike, the *rest* of you. I work . . . for a living . . . I work . . . And I can't just. Get up. And go to rehab . . . What am I suppose to tell my boss? What am I suppose to tell my neighbors? That I'm just. "Taking a trip to rehab? See you in three months??"

BARBARA

(Close) Lillie Anne, for two hundred thousand dollars. You tell your boss and your neighbors whatever the fuck you want to tell them.

(Adlean, smoking, raises her hand.)

Adlean?

ADLEAN

(Smoking, upset) Why the hell would you give me cancer?

(Beat.
    Barbara's cell phone beeps. Barbara looks at it. It's a text message. She reads it.)

BARBARA

The director needs me to make sure that there will be no family problems after the movie comes out. And that you all will have actually *truly* been through rehab and can talk about that experience . . . The director wants a bunch of Oscars . . . And I want a bunch of money and fame. Now ask yourself, what the fuck do you want.

(Marie raises her hand.)

Yes, Marie?

MARIE

(Serious) I want to know, who told you about my minor crack habit?

(Silence.
They all look to Marie.
Barbara's phone begins ringing.
She puts it on vibrate.)

BARBARA

I want an answer and I want an answer now. You know what I can do. You know what I'm capable of. Don't fuck with me.

(They look to Barbara and realize. She has a brand new addiction.
Silence.
Except for the vibrating.
Barbara answers the phone.)

(Addict) Yes. Hello? . . . Yes . . . Hi . . . Yes I'm still here with them . . . Yes, I've read them the letter . . . I think they are seriously considering it . . . I've told them . . . Everything . . . Oh . . . Right . . . I forgot that part . . . Hold on a second . . .

(She looks to her completely dumbfounded siblings.)

(To siblings) Um . . . there is one more thing . . . you should know . . . In order to make my memoirs really real . . . really authentic . . . and *believable* . . . The studio decided . . . to make our family—

(Black.)

EPILOGUE

The Oscars.
  Oscar theme music.
  Thunderous applause.

FAMOUS ACTOR'S VOICE-OVER
Thank you, I've been given the distinguished honor of presenting the last award tonight . . . The nominees for Best Picture
are, *THE MOVIE WITH NOTHING BUT WHITE PEOPLE
IN IT ABOUT A MENTALLY CHALLENGED ADULT.*

(Thunderous applause.)

*THE MOVIE WITH NOTHING BUT WHITE PEOPLE IN
IT ABOUT A MENTALLY CHALLENGED ADULT DURING
WORLD WAR TWO.*

(Thunderous applause.)

THE MOVIE WITH NOTHING BUT WHITE PEOPLE IN IT ABOUT A MENTALLY CHALLENGED ADULT DURING WORLD WAR TWO DONE WITH ENGLISH ACCENTS.

(Thunderous applause.)

And finally, *BARBECUE.*

(Thunderous applause.)

And the winner of the Oscar for Best Picture goes to . . .

(Sound of an envelope opening.)

(Sheer joy) Oh my god!! *BARBECUE*!!!!!

(Cue soundtrack theme song!!
Thunderous applause.
The black movie stars and Black Movie Star Barbara make their way onstage. They each hold an Oscar.
They are done up for the Gods. They shine and sparkle almost to the point of appearing to be fully airbrushed. Not a flaw in sight.
Black Movie Star Barbara, dressed to kill, raises her Best Picture Oscar in the air.)

BLACK MOVIE STAR BARBARA

I told myself I wasn't going to cry . . . First giving honor to God— I mean my agent and manager—sorry . . . And the whole team at ELOMENOPEA. When I initially read Barbara's memoir I knew from the first page that I had to make this movie. And then I met her . . . Wow . . . Wow . . . Wow we never thought something like this would happen. This has been a night I will remember for the rest of my— Wow . . . This movie began with the brave journey of one magnificent woman and her amazing family.

(She motions offstage.
The white family make their way onstage . . . They look star-struck by a Mack Truck and obviously have been styled and dressed by

someone who has no idea about their real life. To a person, they are completely trashed.

Thunderous applause.)

(To the dumbfounded white family) Thank you for sharing your stories from the bowels of your drug and alcohol addiction. I want to thank the Academy and all the tremendously brave actors up here on this stage with me tonight. We took a chance yall and told a story no one believed anyone would ever come see and we ended up here! Not in my wildest dreams did I ever think this could come true. Thank you. Thank you all.

(Black Movie Star Barbara brings White Barbara close.)

Barbara, this is *your* night. This is *your* family's night.

(Black Movie Star Barbara holds the Oscar out to White Barbara who touches it warmly and Black Movie Star Barbara gracefully removes it from White Barbara's touch.)

(Seamlessly continuing) Your story has inspired everyone in this room tonight. And I want to, from the bottom of my heart, once again, thank my agents, for sending me your memoirs at a time when most of you know I, myself, was going through some tough times. Thank you Academy, thank you Seth and Manny. And lastly, thank you, God.

(Thunderous applause.
    She steps back and motions for White Barbara to say a few words.
    Like a deer in headlights, White Barbara steps forward.
    She opens her mouth to speak.
    And.
    Oscar exit music!!!
    Fade to black.)

END OF PLAY

BOOTYCANDY

To Lizzie B, my granny

Bootycandy received its world premiere at Woolly Mammoth Theatre Company (Howard Shalwitz, Artistic Director; Jeffrey Herrmann, Managing Director) in Washington, DC, on May 30, 2011. It was directed by the author; the set design was by Tom Kamm, the costume design was by Kate Turner-Walker, the lighting design was by Colin K. Bills and the sound design was by Lindsay Jones. The production stage manager was William E. Cruttenden III. The cast was:

ACTOR 1	Jessica Frances Dukes
ACTOR 2	Phillip James Brannon
ACTOR 3	Laiona Michelle
ACTOR 4	Lance Coadie Williams
ACTOR 5	Sean Meehan

Bootycandy was subsequently produced at the Wilma Theater (Blanka Zizka, Artistic Director; James Haskins, Managing Director) in Philadelphia, PA, on May 15, 2013. It was directed by the author; the set and costume design was by Clint Ramos, the lighting design was by Drew Billiau and the sound design was by Lindsay Jones; the production stage manager was Patreshettarlini Adams. The cast was:

ACTOR 1	Jocelyn Bioh
ACTOR 2	Phillip James Brannon
ACTOR 3	Benja Kay Thomas
ACTOR 4	Lance Coadie Williams
ACTOR 5	Ross Beschler

Bootycandy was produced at Playwrights Horizons (Tim Sanford, Artistic Director; Leslie Marcus, Managing Director) in New York City, on September 10, 2014. It was directed by the author; the set and costume design was by Clint Ramos, the lighting design was by Japhy Weideman and the sound design was by Lindsay Jones; the production stage manager was Marisa Levy. The cast was:

ACTOR 1	Jessica Frances Dukes
ACTOR 2	Phillip James Brannon
ACTOR 3	Benja Kay Thomas
ACTOR 4	Lance Coadie Williams
ACTOR 5	Jesse Pennington

CHARACTERS

ACTOR 1 (black woman, 20–30):
Young Black Mom, Adella, Big Shirley, Writer 1, Young
Sibling, Intifada

ACTOR 2 (black man, 20–30):
Sutter

ACTOR 3 (black woman, 30–40):
Eudarrie, Lucy, Writer 2, Middle-Aged Mother, Genitalia

ACTOR 4 (black man, 30–40):
Reverend Benson, Writer 3, Stepfather, Larry, Old Granny

ACTOR 5 (white man, 20–40):
Roy, Clint, Moderator, Officiant, White Man

ACT ONE

Bootycandy (1970s)
Dreamin in Church (1980s)
Genitalia (1980s)
Drinks and Desire (1990s)
Mug (2000s)
Conference (Present Day)

ACT TWO

Happy Meal (1980s)
Ceremony (1990s)
Last Gay Play (2000s)
Prison (Present Day)
iPhone (Present Day)

ACT ONE

SCENE 1

Bootycandy

A Young Black Mom dresses her young son, Sutter, who stands in his underwear, holding a children's dictionary.

SUTTER

Mommy where are we going?

YOUNG BLACK MOM

I'm going to the department store and then I'm taking you to the barbershop to get a haircut . . .

SUTTER

I don't want a haircut

YOUNG BLACK MOM

It's not about what you want . . . you need a haircut . . .

SUTTER

Why do I have to get a haircut every time you say I gotta get a haircut?

YOUNG BLACK MOM

Because I'm the mama. And you're the son. Period.

SUTTER

Mommy what's a period?

YOUNG BLACK MOM

What you put at the end of a sentence why?

SUTTER

Because I had my ink pen burst in my pants the other day and the boys said that I had my period and I didn't understand what they meant *(Whispering)* but Mommy I think the period also means something else besides what you put at the end of a sentence.

(Silence.)

YOUNG BLACK MOM

Look it up . . . that's what I bought you that dictionary for.

SUTTER

I did look it up.

YOUNG BLACK MOM

And what did it say?

SUTTER

It said what you put at the end of a sentence.

YOUNG BLACK MOM

Well that's what I just said . . . did you remember to pull your-self back and wash?

SUTTER

Yes ma'am Mommy why do I pull myself back and wash?

YOUNG BLACK MOM

Because you're not circumcised, Sutter.

SUTTER

Circus?!! We going to the CIRCUS???!!!

YOUNG BLACK MOM

Naw we ain't goin to no damn circus, calm down! You have to pull yourself back and wash because you have to keep your bootycandy clean.

SUTTER

Mommy why do you and Granny call my dick bootycandy?

YOUNG BLACK MOM

It's not called a dick who told you that?

SUTTER

Nobody.

YOUNG BLACK MOM

It's called a bootycandy you too young to be calling it a dick don't let me hear you say that again have you lost your mind in real life?

SUTTER

But why do you and Granny call it a bootycandy?

YOUNG BLACK MOM

I don't know I guess because it's the Candy to the Booty!!

SUTTER

So can I lick it?

(Silence.)

YOUNG BLACK MOM

No.

SUTTER

Mommy what's a blowjob?

(Silence.)

YOUNG BLACK MOM

Look it up.

SUTTER

I did.

YOUNG BLACK MOM

And?

SUTTER

It wasn't in there.

YOUNG BLACK MOM

Then it must not be a word right, Sutter? So you should not say thangs that ain't words.

SUTTER

Well Alessa next door wrote me a letter and told me she wanted to give me a blowjob.

(Silence.)

YOUNG BLACK MOM

Alessa needs her ass beat . . . don't let me hear you say that no more.

SUTTER

Why?

YOUNG BLACK MOM

Because I said so and it ain't a word you looked it up didn't you and you didn't find it so I just told you that means it ain't a word so don't say it.

SUTTER

Mommy I still don't know why do I have to pull myself back and wash?

YOUNG BLACK MOM

I just told you because if you don't your bootycandy will get dirty down there.

SUTTER

Then what?

YOUNG BLACK MOM

Then you'll die from dirt and your dick'll fall off!!

(Silence.)

Where's your hat, Sutter?

SUTTER

In my pocket . . .

YOUNG BLACK MOM

Put it on your head

SUTTER

It's ugly.

YOUNG BLACK MOM

It's not ugly . . . it's cold outside . . . you wanna freeze to death and be hackin and coughin all night so that I'll have to be running you down to the hospital . . . who you tryin to be cute for . . . Alessa? . . . You can't be cute and warm too put that hat on your head boy that's what I bought it for.

(Sutter puts the ugly hat on his head.)

SUTTER

What store we going to first?

YOUNG BLACK MOM

Value City.

SUTTER

Goody they got that new Jackson Five tape recorder!!

YOUNG BLACK MOM

I don't want you to touch nothing you ain't fixin to buy . . . cuz why?

SUTTER

Cuz everything I touch turn to shit.

YOUNG BLACK MOM

Right.

SUTTER

When we get there I'm going to the toy department I won't touch nothin I promise.

YOUNG BLACK MOM

And when I come looking for you I want to be able to find you I don't wanna have to search that whole store all day for you I got too many things to do today . . . okay . . . you ready?

SUTTER

Yes ma'am.

YOUNG BLACK MOM

Give me your hand . . . and I hope I don't have tell you when we get into this store to please don't show your black ass . . . do I?

SUTTER

No ma'am.

YOUNG BLACK MOM

Because why?

SUTTER

Because if I show my black ass then that means you gonna have to show your black ass.

YOUNG BLACK MOM

And what?

SUTTER

Your black ass is bigger . . .

YOUNG BLACK MOM

That's right . . . let's go.

SCENE 2

Dreamin in Church

We discover Reverend Benson behind a pulpit in an elaborate floor-length robe.

REVEREND BENSON

church
the last time i spoke to you
we was talkin bout the I HEARD FOLK
and we agreed
that these I HEARD FOLK
loved to always come round us
whisperin
guess what
I HEARD

and we also agreed
that we had a lot of them I HEARD FOLK

ratt heah
in oura church

nah what i didn't tell you last time
was that these I HEARD FOLK
don't always
whispah
they sometimes write
and many of them have written me over the past few weeks
bout somethin that THEY HEARD
ya see when all the I HEARD FOLK get togetha on somethin
then it becomes
THEY HEARD
and that's what i wanna discuss today
church
WHAT
THEY HEARD

so somebody wake up Deacon Floyd and Sista Smith
somebody reach ova and tap Brotha Turner
and pinch Mother Carter and her three children
cos i'm liable to say somethin they don't wanna heah
i'm liable to put my foot down in somethin
that don't smell too fresh or feel just right
cos the THEY HEARD FOLK are fit
(as some might say)
FIT
TO BE READ

(Reverend Benson puts on reading glasses and reads a letter.)

"dear Rev. Benson
because you are in charge of oura house of gawd
we feel that it is only ratt
that you know bout what is goin on
in oura church home"

"we know for a fact that there are a least
a half dozen"

"sexually
perverted"

"young men
who on a regular basis
sang gawd's praises
in oura church choir"

"these young men have been seen
givin each otha knowin looks
holdin each othas hands
hangin round with certain"

"misfits"

"and
at times
kissin inside certain"

"bars"

"we realize that some of them
don't come from the best of families
some of them ain't even gat
a father round like they need
nor any type of a real motha fo that matter
but they must be put ratt
or gotten rid of
all togetha"

"cos gawd don't llow no sin folk
in the kingdom

so we shouldn't llow that kind
in oura church"

"we know you will understand
Rev. Benson
and you will do the
gawd-fearin
ratt thang
to do"

nah the THEY HEARD FOLK
almost never
sign they names
to nothin
and when they do
they sign
somethin lak
"anonymous"
or
"concerned worshipah"
or
"yo brotha in gawd"

but this particular letter is signed

"the folks
who pay yo salary"

(Reverend Benson folds the letter and takes his glasses off.)

nah ya see church
RUMORS
git started
RUMORS
get goin

once the I HEARD FOLK
change into the THEY HEARD FOLK
and from this letter
i take it that
some folk
are concerned
that some of oura
choirboys
are a little

"freaky"

some folk
are worried
that some of oura
choirboys
are a little

"twisted"

cos they
at times
smile
at one anotha
cos they
at times
have a little
look see
at one anotha
What the Man say?
"You can't make no connection
With a screw
And another screw"

What he say?
"You need a Screw

And a
NUT!!!!!!!!"

So church
RUMORS
that's what these THEY HEARD FOLK do
RUMORS
that's how these THEY HEARD FOLK
function
but what you might not know church
is that some of these THEY HEARD FOLK
are tryin to start up new
RUMORS
round MY doorstep
peepin in my windows
tryin to see who i'm with
cos i ain't don took me no wife
some of these THEY HEARD FOLK lak to say
"Reverend!!!
when you gon get hitched"
some of these THEY HEARD FOLK
lak to say
"Rev!!!!"
"who you been seein"
"what you been doin"
"how you been doin it"
"when you been doin it"
"WHERE is yo NUTT!!!!"

and i just wanna say
WHAT
I do
HOW
I do it

and the WHO WHERE and WHEN of it
that's MY bizness

Nah you see Church
This heah is one of dose
What what what what what what
What the woman on the TV say . . .
One of dose
Teachable Moments

How that ol jingle jangle spiritual go
What it say?
"sometimes you feel like a Nut!"
And What?!!!
"sometimes you don't!"

i want you to have a look see
ratt nah
church
at what yo reverend IS
SIT UP!!!!!
and take a look see
at WHO yo reverend IS

(Reverend Benson pulls up the hem of his robe and reveals he is wearing beautiful high-heeled shoes.)

i got my heels on today church
my high heel shoes

(Reverend Benson pulls out a glamorous wig from behind the pulpit and places it on his head.)

got my wig too, church
my special wig

(Reverend Benson pulls out a purse from behind the pulpit.)

got my lipstick
got my rouge
and got my blush

Nah some of yall bout to GET UP

i see some of yall
gatherin ya thangs togetha
ready to run fo the hills
ready to fly outta my sight
but befo you
GET UP

let me tell you one mo thang
i'm tired
of creepin round

i'm tired
of sneakin round

i'm TIRED
watchin every which way I turn
lookin to see who lookin in my direction

i'm tired
of playin that game

i'm tired
of foolin with you all

i'm SICK
and i'm TIRED

nah some of yall lookin at me
as if to say
well nah Rev.
what you gon do nah?
nah that you don up and said it all
are you gon be a sissy nah
are you gon be a faggot nah
are you gon be a flamin queen nah
well i wanta let you know

yo words
can't TOUCH me
yo words
can't REACH me
i'm too HIGH nah
cos i gat the word of GAWD
deep down inside my soul
to protect me
and see me through ALLLL this mess
GAWD'S word is FIRE
SHUT UP IN MY BONES

so if you think i'm flamin nah
take a closer look see
cos i'm on FIIIIYAAAAHH

Yes lawd
nah back to this letter
from the THEY HEARD FOLK
i just wanna say one thang
can I
can I park here fo a moment?
I'm gon park heah for ONE MOMENT
cuz if there's anybody in this heah church
that knows what JESUS

must've felt lak
back there in Galilee
it's these heah
choirboys
ya see
they know
what it feels lak
to be
looked at
to be buked
and scorned
lak Jesus was

so befo ya start
recommendin
who should be put outta
this heah church
you oughta
check yo self
against my JESUS
you oughta
check yo self
against my GAWD

See yall wanna go git yo quick fix
fo what ya see in THEM

(Reverend Benson sing-speaks the rest.
    The SPIRIT has REACHED HIM.)

But MY GAWD
MY, MY
MY, MY, MY
MY, MMY
MMY, MMY, MMY

MY, MY, MY
MY GAWD
WILL FIX YA UP RATT
and i wanna tell all you
CHOIRBOYS
up in heah

you ain't gotta be afraid
of who you are
you ain't gotta be afraid
of what you do

you ain't gatta be afraid!!!!!!

how ya walk
how ya talk
what ya wear
the curl in yo hair
you ain't gatta be afraid!!!!

how ya twirl
how ya whirl
and how ya swirl
cos the I HEARD FOLK
And the THEY HEARD FOLK
will always be sittin around
speakin in tongues
signifi-in
stirrin up RUMORS
runnin from YOU
ta git they FIX
but you ain't gotta be afraid
of alllllll that MESS
Cos lak the lady with the money and the tv show say
THIS is a Teachable Moment
CHURCH

My GAWD tol me
say Rev. Benson
REVEREND
BENSON
Say You need to TELL ALLLL THE CHOIRBOYS up in heah
if ya feel lak SNAPPIN sometimes
up and down and round again
THAT'S ALLLRIGHT

if ya feel lak FLIPPIN yo wrist sometimes
as if ta say
"gon gurrlll gon"
THAT'S ALLLLRIGHT

i feel lak i might as well just let loose church
GOOD GAWD ALMIGHTY
if ya feel lak DRESSIN UP sometimes

(Reverend Benson undoes his robe and reveals that he is wearing a divine dress.)

THAT'S
ALLLLLLLLLLLLLLLLLLLLLLLLLLLLLLLLLLLLLLLLLL
LLLLLL
RIGHT

cos lak the song says
in RUPAUL 19-93-72-24
SASHAY
SHANTE
SASHAY
SHANTE
SHANTE
SHANTE
TURN TO THE LEFT

TURN TO THE RIGHT
WERK
YOOOOOOOUUUUUU BETTA WERK!!!

SO FO ALL THE CHOIRBOYS UP IN HEAH
AND MORE THAN A FEW OF THE CHOIRGIRLS TOO!!!!

SOMEBODY needs ta
STAND UP
and say "Rev. Benson
I'M WITH YA"
SOMEBODY needs ta
RIIIIIIIIIIISE UP
and say "Rev. Benson
WERK ON"
SOMEBODY needs ta
JUMP UP
and SAY "AAAAAAAMEN"
AMEN
AMEN
AMEN
AMEN

(Reverend Benson continues repeating "amen" for the rest of his life.)

SCENE 3

Genitalia

A landline phone conversation.

EUDARRIE

How you gon go n name that chile Genitalia fool?

ADELLA

I ain't changin her last name ta no fool who tol you that?

EUDARRIE

I'm callin you a fool cuz you bout ta name that baby Genitalia, fool!

ADELLA

I like it it has a right nice ring to it.

> EUDARRIE

Genitalia?!!

> ADELLA

Yeah! Genitalia Lakeitha Shalama Abdul

> EUDARRIE

That ain't no kinda name fo no chile soundin lak somethin you order to eat you don already put those other two you gat ta shame

> ADELLA

What about Avis and Cicada ain't nuthin wrong wit they names what you talkin?

> EUDARRIE

One name afta a rent-a-car n otha name afta a blind insect

> ADELLA

So?

> EUDARRIE

So yo name is Adella. How you git ta com up ta namin some-body Geni—

(Beep.)

—hold on for a second gul let me see who this is on my otha line.

(Click.)

Hello?

> BIG SHIRLEY

Gul have you heard what yo sista bout ta name that—

> EUDARRIE

You know I did I'm talkin ta the heifa ratt nah.

BIG SHIRLEY

Well try n talk some sense inta her hell she might as well gon head and name it vagina.

EUDARRIE

(*Laughing*) Thas exactly what I was about to tell her but she don't wanna listen ta nobody n on top of that she gon tack on som Shalaya Shaluka Muslim shit o somethin ain't nobody never heard of n you n me bof know she don't know a bit mo bout Muslim than shit—chile hold on let me get her off the line—

BIG SHIRLEY

Tell her I say lay offa that pipe!

(*Click.*)

EUDARRIE

Adella you still there?

ADELLA

Yeah who dat on yo other line?

EUDARRIE

It's Big Shirley callin me cuz she heard you been consultin with Daffy Duck n the rest of the loony toon gang ova what ta name yo chile.

ADELLA

Yall can say what ya wont but I lak the sound of it

EUDARRIE

And I like the sound of fool, FOOL! Let me gon and see what Shirley talkin bout you need ta take a lil time out n think about what it means to be puttin all that on a lil chile who don't know nuthin n can't tell you ta go ta hell fo namin it that, I'll call you in a bit you still goin ta the bingo?

ADELLA

I might try n git on ova there I was thinkin bout goin down ta the boat play me some quarter slots

EUDARRIE

Call me fo you leave . . . "Genitalia" . . . you a fool I see that nah . . .

(Click.)

Yeah Shirley gul I'm back

BIG SHIRLEY

You find out what she sniffin?

EUDARRIE

I don't know honey but it's strong whatsineva it is

BIG SHIRLEY

(Laughing) Nah gul you never finish tellin me bout how she showed her ass out when yall was bringin yo Aint Katie back from down Bama did Adella eva start the car back up, Eudarrie?

EUDARRIE

Naw! Not at first!! She gon tell me that she didn't have nough gas left to git me home and if I wasn't gonna split Sista's money with her I could at least come up offa some money from my own pocket for a lil bit of gas.

BIG SHIRLEY

What?? Outta yo own pocket??!!

EUDARRIE

That's when I looked ova and seen that the tank was reading half full, but she gon say that that means it's half empty, not half full.

BIG SHIRLEY

You know she pulled that same shit with me befo when I had
had her to take me to go git my carton of Virginia Slims menthols cross the river.

EUDARRIE

We five fucking blocks from my curbside and she tryin to give
me some mess bout gas.

BIG SHIRLEY

She told me I owed her five dollars for taking me cross the gatdamn river—

EUDARRIE

All the time we racin down the street she screamin bout how
I'm sittin on a whole heap of money I got from salein that ol
piece of house of mine after Judge passed.

BIG SHIRLEY

I told her she can kiss the five-dollar side of my ass crack . . .

EUDARRIE

Nah, I ain't git no helluva lot of nuthin for that house after it
was all said and done

BIG SHIRLEY

It ain't none of her bizness how much you gat.

EUDARRIE

It wasn't none of her bizness how much I gat from it in the first
place.

BIG SHIRLEY

That's yo money!!

EUDARRIE

It's my money!!

> **BIG SHIRLEY**

Xactly.

> **EUDARRIE**

That's xactly what I told her.

> **BIG SHIRLEY***

That's yo money! And if you wanna take it and throw it up a wild hog's ass and yell SUEY!!

> **EUDARRIE***

It's my money! And if I wanna take it and throw it up a wild hog's ass and yell SUEY!!

> **BIG SHIRLEY**

You Will!!

> **EUDARRIE**

I Will!!

> **BIG SHIRLEY**

Because It's Yo Money!

> **EUDARRIE**

Because It's My Money!—

(Beep.)

> **BIG SHIRLEY**

—hold on fo a second gul that's my otha line.

(Click.)

Hello?

> **LUCY**

GUL SHE NAMIN HER CHILE PUSSY!!

BIG SHIRLEY

(Laughing) Lucy you a fool she namin it Genitalia how you com up with PUSSY!

LUCY

Dats what I heard

BIG SHIRLEY

Well you heard wrong, I'm talkin ta her sista Eudarrie ratt nah hold on

(Click.)

(Laughing) Chile my sista Lucy on my other line so let me get off this phone you goin ta the bingo tonight o you gon try ta git ta the boat?

EUDARRIE

Adella talkin bout tryin ta go ta the boat but my number came through last night so I got me little bit of cash n I don't know if I wanna be losin it all on som slot machines so . . . ah don't know . . . but I'm sure I'll end up at one place o the otha . . .

BIG SHIRLEY

Give me a call fo you go I might join ya . . .

EUDARRIE

Alright chile, you take care, I talk ta you soon . . .

(Click.)

BIG SHIRLEY

Yeah gul, Genitalia . . . Genitalia somethin somethin Muslim

LUCY

Lawd sweet Jesus. She don lost all of her mind!

SCENE 4

Drinks and Desire

Sutter and Roy at various bars throughout the city.

                                        SUTTER

So what do you think?

(Silence.)

                                        ROY

Sutter, I don't know

                                        SUTTER

Okay Roy

                                        ROY

I mean . . . I don't know when

I know I
I would like to try

SUTTER

Try what?

ROY

I don't know
something

SUTTER

What?

ROY

I don't know Sutter

SUTTER

What?!

ROY

I don't know
something!!

SUTTER

. . . When?

ROY

I.
Do. Not.
Know.

SUTTER

Okay fine. Roy.

(Pause.)

> ROY

. . . What would you want . . .
to do . . .
. . . Huh?

(Silence.)

> SUTTER

I would want . . .
to put your dick in my mouth
and suck on the tip of it gently
then lick the shaft
and maybe
maybe
kiss your balls
then deep throat you
. . . slowly . . . Roy.

(Silence.)

> ROY

. . . When?

> SUTTER

Now.

> ROY

We can't . . . do it here . . .

> SUTTER

Let's go somewhere
your place

> ROY

No

SUTTER

Why not?
No one's there

ROY

I'd
I'd wanna be able to leave
if I didn't like

SUTTER

You'd like it

ROY

. . . Well I'd

SUTTER

You'd. Like. It.

(Pause.)

You need more time?

ROY

No I
I actually don't need more time
I've thought about this a lot Sutter

SUTTER

I know

ROY

An awful lot

SUTTER

I know

ROY

I thought about what if you were to

                              SUTTER
No

                              ROY
I know

                              SUTTER
No wigs

                              ROY
I know

(*Pause.*)

. . . Would you let me fuck you?

                              SUTTER
Yes.

                              ROY
Without a condom

                              SUTTER
. . . Maybe

                              ROY
Could I cum?

                              SUTTER
Where

                              ROY
Inside you

                              SUTTER
Where Roy

ROY

. . . Your mouth

SUTTER

Yes

ROY

Your ass

SUTTER

. . . No . . .
Maybe . . .

(Pause.)

ROY

. . . Okay

SUTTER

What?

ROY

Okay

SUTTER

What?!!

ROY

Let's go

SUTTER

Where?

ROY

Your place

SUTTER

Okay

ROY

Okay

SUTTER

Okay

ROY

Let's

SUTTER

Wait.

(Pause.)

ROY

What

SUTTER

What do you wanna do?

ROY

I told you I don't

SUTTER

Say it

ROY

I don't really—

SUTTER

Say. It.

ROY

. . . I want you to ride my dick

SUTTER

Your dick

ROY

. . . My dick

SUTTER

Your big dick

ROY

I want you to ride my big dick
and let me fuck deep inside you
I wanna fuck your face
I wanna fuck your ass

SUTTER

Do you wanna fuck me?

ROY

. . .

SUTTER

Do you wanna fuck me?

ROY

Yes.

SUTTER

Will you suck my dick?

ROY

Yes.

SUTTER

Will you suck my nipples?

ROY

Yes

SUTTER

Will you eat out my ass?

ROY

Yes

SUTTER

And kiss me

ROY

No

(Pause.)

. . . Let's go.

SUTTER

. . . Let's go.

(Dark.
    Then.
    Light.)

ROY

I I
I've been uh
having thoughts

SUTTER

About what

ROY

You

SUTTER

. . . And?

ROY

. . . And other

SUTTER

What?

ROY

Men

(Pause.)

SUTTER

About me and other men or

ROY

Yes

SUTTER

Or you and other men

ROY

Yes

SUTTER

What?

ROY

About you and me
and other
men

SUTTER

. . . Fucking

ROY

Yeah

SUTTER

You?

ROY

Yeah

SUTTER

About other men fucking you

ROY

Yeah

SUTTER

Okay

ROY

And you . . .
fucking me . . .

(Silence.)

SUTTER

I was sixteen

ROY

What?

SUTTER

My first time

ROY

Oh

SUTTER

You wanted to know didn't you

ROY

Yeah
. . . Sixteen?

SUTTER

Yeah

ROY

Did it hurt

SUTTER

Yeah

ROY

Pain

SUTTER

Pleasure . . . pain
Pleasure . . . pain
Pleasure . . . pain
Pleasure

ROY

. . . Who was

SUTTER

You want me to say my father

ROY

. . . No

SUTTER

You want me to say my uncle
Your uncle?

ROY

What?

SUTTER

It was your uncle

ROY

What?!

SUTTER

(Laughing) Just kidding

ROY

(Laughing) Okay

SUTTER

Actually it was your father.

(Silence.
    Silence.)

I wanted

ROY

SHUT—

SUTTER

I wanted it
I asked for it
I begged for him to.

(Pause.)

You knew

(Pause.)

ROY

I didn't

SUTTER

. . .

ROY

I didn't know
for sure.

SUTTER

My sister knew
I told her

ROY

. . . When

SUTTER

The day you married her
and she said
she knew

ROY

. . . . I'm sorry

(Roy reaches out.)

SUTTER

Don't touch
please

ROY

Okay

SUTTER

. . . Thanks . . .

ROY

What?

SUTTER

Thank you.

(Silence.)

People
think
that we're together
here

ROY

I know

SUTTER

That doesn't bother you

ROY

Who gives a shit

SUTTER

That doesn't

ROY

No

SUTTER

You don't

ROY

No!

(Pause.)

I'm straight

(Pause.)

SUTTER

I know

(Dark.
   Then.
   Light.)

Please.

ROY

Okay.

SUTTER

Don't. Call. Anymore.

ROY

Okay

SUTTER

Don't. Write.

ROY

Okay

SUTTER

Anymore

ROY

Okay

SUTTER

You're straight

ROY

I know

SUTTER

Stay that way

(Silence.)

ROY

You tried once.
A girl.

SUTTER

Once.

ROY

Who

SUTTER

High school

ROY

Who?!

SUTTER

Nobody
you'd know

ROY

Who?!!

SUTTER

Tamara

ROY

Green?

SUTTER

Green.

ROY

No

SUTTER

Once.

ROY

And

SUTTER

Awful

ROY

. . . I tried

SUTTER

What?!

ROY

Tamara

SUTTER

Oh

ROY

Awful

(Laughter.)

SUTTER

Remember Kevin

ROY

Her brother

SUTTER

Yes

ROY

Nice

SUTTER

Ass

ROY

Yes!

(Pause.)

I mean—

SUTTER

Gym class

ROY

Every day

SUTTER

Every. Day.

ROY

Nice

SUTTER

Ass

(Silence.)

ROY

I wanna be your friend
just

SUTTER

Don't. Call.

ROY

Friends

SUTTER

Don't. Write.

ROY

. . . Okay . . .

SUTTER

They need you

(Roy reaches.)

Don't.
Touch. Roy.

(Dark.
    Then.
    Light.)

ROY

If anybody found out

SUTTER

I know

ROY

Crazy

SUTTER

Yep . . .

ROY

Lose so much

SUTTER

Yeah

ROY

Definitely your sister

SUTTER

Yep.
Definite—

ROY

Why'd you come?

SUTTER

. . . You called . . .

(Pause.)

ROY

I don't
I want you to know something

SUTTER

I know

ROY

You're not
the person
I wanna spend the rest of my life with

I can't make that type of
com
com
commitment

SUTTER

I know

ROY

Your sister
I love her

SUTTER

Ditto

ROY

We haven't touched since

SUTTER

You and my sister?

ROY

You and I.

SUTTER

Oh

ROY

We haven't touched since

SUTTER

That night

ROY

That
night.

(Pause.)

SUTTER

You wrote.

ROY

Yes

SUTTER

I asked you not to

ROY

I called
I wrote
I thought a lot . . . Sutter
was I good?

SUTTER

. . . No.

ROY

. . . No?

SUTTER

No
not as good desired

ROY

Oh

SUTTER

Desired
Desire
was better

(Silence.)

ROY

I don't love you Sutter

SUTTER

I know Roy

ROY

I don't

SUTTER

Yeah

ROY

Really

SUTTER

I know

ROY

Desire

SUTTER

Yes

ROY

Is better
. . . . . . for us

SUTTER

. . . . Yes

(Pause.)

ROY

Stop it.

SUTTER

What

ROY

Stop it

SUTTER

I can't

ROY

Stop

SUTTER

What?!

ROY

Letting me
Needing me
You make me feel
Stop

(Pause.)

SUTTER

I don't love you
either
I never loved you

(Silence.)

ROY

. . . Say it . . .

SUTTER

I never—

ROY

Don't lie

SUTTER

I didn't

ROY

Say it

SUTTER

No

ROY

Say it!

SUTTER

What?

ROY

SAY IT!!

SUTTER

I DON'T!

ROY

You love me Sutter

SUTTER

No

ROY

Say it

SUTTER

. . . Uh-uh . . .

ROY

Fuck you!!
Say it!!

SUTTER

Uh-uh

ROY

You do

SUTTER

Uh-uh

ROY

YOU DO!!!

(Pause.)

SUTTER

. . . . . .
(Crying)
. . . Uh-uh . . .

(Pause.)

ROY

. . . I'm sorry

(Roy reaches out.)

SUTTER

Don't.
Touch Roy.

ROY

I'm sorry

SUTTER

Please

ROY

I'm so—
okay

SUTTER

Thanks

ROY

What?

SUTTER

. . . Thank you.

(Dark.
Then.
Light.
Roy alone.
He waits.
He waits.
He waits.)

SCENE 5

Mug

Clint stands on the street . . . late at night . . . waiting for a bus. Clint looks up and down the street . . . looks at his watch . . . sighs. After a moment, Clint speaks to someone we can't see.

CLINT

. . . . No.

  No.

  No.

  I said no . . .

  Why would you want to do that? . . .

  . . . I mean seriously . . . why would you want to do that? . . . Am I rollin a Lexus here? . . . I'm waiting for the bus . . . it's three A.M. in the morning and I'm waiting for the bus because I only have three dollars and it costs that much just to sit down in a taxi at this time of the night.

. . . Look I got a driver's license, MetroCard and a few maxxed out credit cards . . . mints, lint and three dollars . . . What are you gonna do with that? . . . You know what I'm saying? . . . Don't you have better things to do besides bop me over the head and take my little cash that won't even buy you a beer at the bar down the street there . . . most certainly can't buy you any useable amount of drugs . . .

You would ruin my already bullshit of a night . . . and you'd ruin your life . . . because you'd have to kill me . . . That's the only way you'll take anything of mine . . .

And I'm certainly planning to either take you with me or take a large piece of you with me . . . so the cops would eventually find you . . . either here dead next to me or by doing some tests on whatever chunks of you I have between my dead fists or my dead teeth . . . they'd do DNA tests blood tests what have you tests and since you probably have a record already it won't take them long to find out who you are and where your mother lives because you obviously still live with her or maybe just maybe with your baby's mama and they'd track you down in a week maybe a month maybe a little later and they'd take you to court and whatever you don't confess to they'll prove to the jury you did it anyway . . . you'd go to jail for murder this time . . . a few other charges . . . end up back where you just got out of what two-three weeks ago? . . .

But this time that guy you fucked with when he first got there has now come up n gained weight been working out waiting for you to come back . . . he'll beat the living shit out of you and then stab a plastic man-made utensil in your eye or your neck or up your ass or maybe in that space from where I took that chuck of your flesh . . . wherever . . .

And you'd bleed to death thinking something like damn if I'd just left that muthafucka alone at that bus station late that one night I wouldn't be getting numb all over and going to hell right now as this asshole above me stomps my face into the concrete of this jail floor . . .

So . . . why don't you just go home . . . go to sleep . . . wake up . . . go down to . . . Mickey D's . . . the Gap . . . apply for a job . . . and . . . see what happens . . .

Who knows . . . you might make enough to . . . I don't know—start payin child support on your what? Six kids? . . . Even if you start giving support for one of them . . . that's a beginning . . .

Treat your moms to a dinner out . . . a decent pair of "kicks" for yourself that you didn't have to "boost" . . . you might meet a few folks you'd never thought you'd ever hang out with . . . go out for a drink after work . . . shoot the shit . . . leave . . . and realize it's way later than you first thought but you got the last round at the bar with your newfound nondelinquent friends so now you have just three dollars to your name . . .

You remember that you took your medication you bought that unlimited MetroCard yesterday so you're cool . . . you wait for the bus . . . even tho it's late . . . too late for waiting . . . then some kid'll come by you and . . .

. . . Keep right on walkin . . .

Because . . . he's got better things to do with his evening . . . he's just tryin to get home without getting jacked . . . himself . . .

(Silence.)

What's your name?
    Anthony . . . I'm Clint.
    . . . Have a good night, Anthony . . .
    . . . No . . . thank you . . .

(Clint looks at his watch . . . and continues to wait for the bus.)

SCENE 6

Conference

Sutter, a group of black playwrights (all dressed in a variation of Sutter's costume), and a white Moderator sit in a half circle facing the audience.
Long silence.

WRITER 1

. . . I'm sorry—

MODERATOR

Yes.

WRITER 1

I don't understand exactly

MODERATOR

What—

WRITER 1

Why we're here.

MODERATOR

Does anyone want to answer that for Kerry.

WRITER 1

Terry.

MODERATOR

For Terry.

WRITER 2

. . . I don't . . . understand either.

MODERATOR

So there are two of you who have absolutely no idea why you're here.

WRITER 3

Make that three.

SUTTER

Four.

(Pause.)

MODERATOR

. . . None of you have any idea why we're here today?

(Silence.)

(Embarrassed) Well, someone screwed up didn't they?— Um . . . well . . .

WRITER 3

Is this like uh—group?

MODERATOR

A conference.

(Tension.)

WRITER 1

On what?

MODERATOR

Well . . . of course on . . . playwriting—

WRITER 2

Playwriting?

MODERATOR

Yes, you're all—is there a problem—you're all . . . playwrights—

WRITER 3

Is there a . . . theme?

(The Moderator looks at all of them in amazement.)

MODERATOR

Are you serious?

WRITER 3

Do I look serious?

MODERATOR

Yes.

WRITER 2

What. Is the title of this conference—

MODERATOR

The title is . . . Black

                              SUTTER

Black??!!

                              MODERATOR

Fire

                              SUTTER

What??!!

                              MODERATOR

Hot—

                              WRITER 1

Hot?

                              MODERATOR

Emerging—

                              WRITER 3

I've been writing for twenty years.

                              MODERATOR

And Established—

                              WRITER 3

I haven't had a production in twenty years

                              MODERATOR

Unknown—

                              WRITER 2

I won a Pulitzer.

                              MODERATOR

(Genuine) You did, when?

(They look to him in amazement.)

I didn't— That's not in . . . my notes.

SUTTER

Who are you?

MODERATOR

I'm the moderator.

(Pause.)

WRITER 1

Is this a breakout session?

MODERATOR

No.

WRITER 2

So we're the conference? The entire conference?

MODERATOR

Well obviously there's an audience.

(He motions to the live audience and they look at the live audience as if they are seeing them for the first time.
    Silence.)

WRITER 3

(Serious) What the fuck is going on?

MODERATOR

(To live audience) Ladies and gentlemen there's been a slight misunder—

SUTTER

Is this a talkback—

MODERATOR

No it's a conference. You all signed a release form—

WRITER 1

Release from what?!!

MODERATOR

A release form not a re— You were— I'm sorry someone screwed up. This is the part of the conference where we ask you what . . . you're working on. Then we have a Q-and-A

WRITER 2

About what?

MODERATOR

Your work.

WRITER 3

Why?

MODERATOR

Because that's part—this is the part of the conference where that happens—where that is done . . . People talk about—a little about what you're—then

(Silence.)

So what are you all working on, Kerry—uh Terry—O'Malley, by the way I've often wondered, how exactly did you get the name Terry O'Malley—seems odd for a black playwright to have the last name O'Malley how did that come about?

WRITER 1

Slavery.

(Silence.)

MODERATOR

Okay . . . um . . . So what are you working on?

WRITER 1

I'm working on a play about a preacher . . . who comes out of the closet . . .

MODERATOR

Okay

WRITER 1

In front of his congregation . . .

MODERATOR

Okay . . .

WRITER 1

In a dress . . .

MODERATOR

Ohhhkay . . . Well . . . you don't actually think anyone's going to produce that play do you?

WRITER 1

No.

MODERATOR

Good. Um . . .
    (Turns to Writer 2) And you?

WRITER 2

You don't even know my name do you?

MODERATOR

My-ke-le

WRITER 2

Michael.

MODERATOR

Michael. Strange name for a woman.

(Silence.)

Right. What are you working on?

WRITER 2

I'm writing a play about a woman on the phone. With some other women. Talking about pussy.

MODERATOR

What does that have to do with race?

WRITER 2

What does pussy have to do with race?

MODERATOR

What do women on the phone talking about pussy have to do with race?

WRITER 2

Why does it have to have anything to do with race?

MODERATOR

You're a black playwright.

WRITER 2

Yeah.

MODERATOR

And you're just writing a play about a woman on the phone with other women?

WRITER 2

Yeah. And pussy.

MODERATOR

And it has nothing to do with race?

WRITER 2

. . . No.

MODERATOR

Okay.

(Turns to Writer 3) So um . . . I see here that you've changed your name to a symbol.

WRITER 3

Yes, I felt that my parents had given me a European oppressor's name.

MODERATOR

So now you write as just a symbol.

WRITER 3

Yes.

MODERATOR

And what does your symbol symbolize?

WRITER 3

What do you think?

MODERATOR

(Looks at paper) Well . . . to me . . . it looks like . . .
(Examines the paper seriously) Two people fucking?

WRITER 3

Exactly.

MODERATOR

Okay. What are you working on?

WRITER 3

I'm working on a play about two people fucking . . . A man and his brother . . . in-law.

MODERATOR

In a symbolic way.

WRITER 3

No they really fuck each other.

MODERATOR

Oh.

WRITER 3

In the butt.

(Silence.)

They're also best friends.

MODERATOR

Ohhhh . . . Okay . . . now I get it . . . that's really an insightful idea for a play. Great . . .
   (To Sutter) Now Sutter, you've actually had a play done just recently . . . right here on this very stage as a matter of fact.

SUTTER

Yes.

MODERATOR

I saw it . . . the title is slipping my mind, but . . . What was it called?

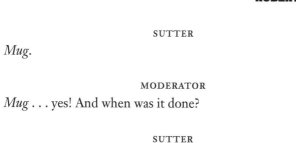

SUTTER

Mug.

MODERATOR

Mug . . . yes! And when was it done?

SUTTER

Ten minutes ago.

MODERATOR

Right . . . Okay. Now that play was about a white man—

SUTTER

It wasn't about a white man—

MODERATOR

It wasn't?

SUTTER

No. It had nothing to do with a white man.

MODERATOR

But . . . I recall a white man being on the stage . . . for the entire play.

SUTTER

So.

MODERATOR

There were no other people onstage with him.

SUTTER

So.

MODERATOR

So your play *Mug*, which only has a white man onstage by himself the entire—

SUTTER

How do you know he was white?

MODERATOR

He wasn't white?

SUTTER

He was a white actor.

MODERATOR

But he wasn't playing a white character?

SUTTER

I'm just saying my play is not about a white man . . . it's about avoiding a mugging . . . the play could've been done with a blue midget . . .

(Pause.)

MODERATOR

So the white actor was actually playing a blue midget and not a white man?

SUTTER

It has nothing to do with a white man. I don't write plays about white people.

MODERATOR

Right . . . right . . . So what are you working on now?

SUTTER

I'm doing rewrites on a piece about how my mother use to call my penis bootycandy.

MODERATOR

(Serious) . . . Did she know you were gay when she called it that?

SUTTER

. . . What? *(Looks to the audience)*

MODERATOR

Booty. Candy. Did she know you were . . .

(He makes a gay gesture. Looks to the audience. Then back to Sutter.)

. . . Nothing.

(Silence.)

WRITER 3

Is there a stipend for this conf—

MODERATOR

It's in your pocket—packet—it should've— It's in the packet that you got—you'll get—

WRITER 1

What is this conference about—

MODERATOR

This conference has been convened to open up the question of the debate that has been the contention of the controversy inside the dialectic surrounding the conundrum while we investigate and raise query into the interrogation on the state of African-American—

WRITER 1

What the fuck are *you* talking about?!!

MODERATOR

The question.

WRITER 2

There's something seriously wrong with you.

MODERATOR

Is that a question?

WRITER 3

(Pointing to the audience) Are those subscribers?!

MODERATOR

(Looking out at the audience) . . . Not for long.

    (Back to the writers) So . . . Each of you seem to have a strong facility with language and structure as well as grappling with some rather provocative issues and risky situations . . . I'm wondering what you are hoping the audience comes away with after seeing your work?

SUTTER

I think the audience should choke.

MODERATOR

Choke?

SUTTER

Asphyxiate.

MODERATOR

To death?

WRITER 1

I don't want them to digest it easily.

WRITER 2

It wasn't easy to write it and it shouldn't be easy to experience it.

WRITER 3

Exactly. It should not melt in yo mouth.

SUTTER

The work should be work.

WRITER 1

After you choke on something and you've struggled to get it down your throat. You can FEEL its presence in the space it went through.

WRITER 2

It lingers there.

WRITER 3

There is a physical memory after one chokes.

WRITER 2

Lingering.

SUTTER

It makes you aware that all chocolate cake . . . ain't the same.

WRITER 1

Some of em gats nutz in em.

WRITER 2

Some of em filled with cream.

WRITER 3

Others topped with cherries.

MODERATOR

Are we talking autoerotic asphyxiation.

WRITERS

Yes.

MODERATOR

Or choking on a big piece of fried chicken neck bone.

WRITERS

Yes!!

(The light and sound changes.
   The writers and Sutter begin to chant:)

WRITERS AND SUTTER

Choke Muthafucka Choke!
Choke Muthafucka Choke!
Choke Muthafucka!
Choke Muthafucka!
Choke Muthafucka Choke!

(Lights and sound change back to normal and we are back at the conference in front of the gathered audience.
   The Moderator begins to choke.)

Breathe.

(He manages to breathe. The Moderator looks out.)

MODERATOR

Let's all take a short . . . Breather.

ACT TWO

SCENE 7

Happy Meal

Seated at the kitchen table.

   A Happy Meal dinner has been eaten.

   A Young Sibling plays with an action figure from a Happy Meal.
A Stepfather looks at horse racing stats in the paper. A teenage son,
Sutter, reads a Jackie Collins novel. A Middle-Aged Mother talks to
no one in particular.

MIDDLE-AGED MOTHER

. . . You know Barbara sits up there at that front desk and thinks
she's runnin shit but she ain't . . . She sits there all damn day
being nosy, in and out of other folks bizness and thinks she's
the head nigga in charge but I had to tell her fat ass today that
she wasn't runnin shit . . . She likes to sit up there and run her
damn mouth all damn day with her nosy ass . . . and like I said,
I walked right up to her today and had to put her in her place

. . . I had to just let her know, you know, that she wasn't running shit . . . She sit right up there, jabbering on that damn phone for half a damn hour, looking like she's in charge of something but I walked right up to her this morning and said, "Barbara, you ain't runnin shit around here" . . . I told her, I said, "Barbara, you need to know something and I'm gonna be the one to tell you" . . . I looked her right in the face when I got in today and saw her sitting up there with her chest poked out with that damn raggedy ass blue sweater she likes to hang across the back her damn chair . . . and I said, "Barbara, there is something that needs to be said so I'm gonna be the one to say it" . . . . . . I went right into work this morning and saw her sitting there and marched my fat ass right up into her face and said, "Barbara—"

TEENAGE SUTTER

A man followed me home today.

MIDDLE-AGED MOTHER

"—you ain't the one running shit around—"
(To Teenage Sutter) What?

TEENAGE SUTTER

A man tried to follow me home today.

MIDDLE-AGED MOTHER

What are you talking about?

TEENAGE SUTTER

A man—

MIDDLE-AGED MOTHER

What man?

TEENAGE SUTTER

I don't know his name.

(Silence.)

MIDDLE-AGED MOTHER

What was you doing?

TEENAGE SUTTER

. . . Nothing.

MIDDLE-AGED MOTHER

You had to be doing something for some man to try and follow you home. Ain't no man ever tried to follow me home.

TEENAGE SUTTER

I was at the library.

MIDDLE-AGED MOTHER

Doing what?

TEENAGE SUTTER

. . . Reading.

MIDDLE-AGED MOTHER

Reading what?

TEENAGE SUTTER

A book.

MIDDLE-AGED MOTHER

You was just sitting up in a library reading a book and some man got up and decided to try to follow you home.

TEENAGE SUTTER

Yes ma'am.

MIDDLE-AGED MOTHER

He didn't say nothing.

TEENAGE SUTTER

No ma'am.

MIDDLE-AGED MOTHER

He just started following you home.

TEENAGE SUTTER

Yes ma'am.

MIDDLE-AGED MOTHER

. . . Well you had to have done something for him to start following you home. Folks don't just up and start following teenage boys home just for no reason. You had to have been doing
something to—

TEENAGE SUTTER

I was reading a book in the library. I left the library and he
started following me. I went down the wrong street to trick
him. Then . . . I ran.

MIDDLE-AGED MOTHER

Iran? . . . What Iran got to do with it? Who you know in Iran?

TEENAGE SUTTER

I Ran . . . through someone's backyard . . . I got to our street and
I think I lost him but I know he was trying to follow me home.

(Silence.
    The Middle-Aged Mother looks to the Stepfather.)

STEPFATHER

(Simple fact) You need to take up some sports.

TEENAGE SUTTER

Sports?

STEPFATHER

Wrestlin.

TEENAGE SUTTER

Wrestling.

STEPFATHER

Yeah. Football, wrestlin, something. You need to start doing some sports. You come to this table every night with a book in your hand.

TEENAGE SUTTER

. . . A MAN. Followed me home today—

STEPFATHER

Baseball—

TEENAGE SUTTER

And it wasn't the first time.

(Silence.
The Middle-Aged Mother looks to the Stepfather.)

MIDDLE-AGED MOTHER

(To Teenage Sutter) . . . How many times has this man tried to follow you home?

TEENAGE SUTTER

A few times.

MIDDLE-AGED MOTHER

A few times.

TEENAGE SUTTER

After he put his arms around me . . . while I was waiting for the bus . . . In front of the school. He sometimes comes to the front of the school and waits for me with the other kids and . . . one

day he came over to me and asked me if I was lonely. I said . . .
yes. He said that I didn't have to be lonely. He said he had two
sons and when they get lonely he hugs them. So he asked me if
I needed a hug and I said . . . yes. And he put his arms around
me and asked me if I wanted to come back to his place . . .

(Silence.
The Middle-Aged Mother looks to the Stepfather.)

STEPFATHER

Kung fu.

(Silence.)

TEENAGE SUTTER

. . . He would wait for me after the bus brought us back from
Kings Island. When I was working there over the summer.
Remember? I called you and said I wanted you to come pick
me up? I said there was a man who always waited for me after
the bus left us off at night. And you said to bring my ass home
and quit talking silly. That's the same man.

(Silence.)

MIDDLE-AGED MOTHER

This school year. No musicals.

TEENAGE SUTTER

But they're doing *The Wiz*.

MIDDLE-AGED MOTHER

You are not going to be in no damn *Wiz*.

TEENAGE SUTTER

I've been cast as the Scarecrow already.

MIDDLE-AGED MOTHER

I don't care if you been cast as the Scarecrow's Mama. You are going to walk in there and tell that teacher that you can't do no more musicals because you have to go wrestle . . . or bounce a ball . . . or jump a hurdle.

TEENAGE SUTTER

Michael Jackson played the Scarecrow.

MIDDLE-AGED MOTHER

I don't care if Michael Jackson's Mama played the Scarecrow!

STEPFATHER

(*Simple fact*) You need to start bending your knees when you pick stuff up.

(*Silence.*)

TEENAGE SUTTER

What?

MIDDLE-AGED MOTHER

You don't say "what" to him. This is your father.

TEENAGE SUTTER

Stepfather.

MIDDLE-AGED MOTHER

What??

TEENAGE SUTTER

Nuthin.

STEPFATHER

You need to start bending your knees when you pick stuff up . . . and when you empty your plate in the garbage.

TEENAGE SUTTER

Uh . . . Okay.

MIDDLE-AGED MOTHER

Okay???

TEENAGE SUTTER

(To Stepfather) Yes sir.

STEPFATHER

And you need to stop playing those Whitney Houston albums
. . . And stop talking on the phone for three hours every night
with Brandon about *Star Search*. And start mowing the lawn
twice a week.

MIDDLE-AGED MOTHER

And wash my car.

STEPFATHER

And scrub the bathroom with more Comet.

MIDDLE-AGED MOTHER

And do the dishes without listening to that Culture Club.

STEPFATHER

And take them stickers of DeBarge and Madonna and Prince
and the Jacksons off the side of your bunk bed.

MIDDLE-AGED MOTHER

And stop watching Entertainment Tonight.

STEPFATHER

And stop playing so much Uno.

MIDDLE-AGED MOTHER

And ride your bike around the corner a few times every day.

STEPFATHER

And put that train set together downstairs.

MIDDLE-AGED MOTHER

And stop pretending to conduct a gospel choir in your room with the door closed.

STEPFATHER

And stop making up songs about food.

MIDDLE-AGED MOTHER

And stop taking your little sister out of her top bunk to sleep in your bottom bunk with you every night because you're scare of the dark and then putting her back in her top bunk before we come in and wake you up for school.

STEPFATHER

And stop sitting down to pee.

MIDDLE-AGED MOTHER

And build a snowman for once in your life.

STEPFATHER

And stop playing with my anal beads.

MIDDLE-AGED MOTHER

And learn how to float.

STEPFATHER

And stop jiggling so much when you walk.

MIDDLE-AGED MOTHER

And track some dirt in this house from playing in some field.

STEPFATHER

And learn the difference between a wrench and pliers.

MIDDLE-AGED MOTHER

And stop snapping your bubble gum.

STEPFATHER

And build a tree house out back.

MIDDLE-AGED MOTHER

And feed and walk that dog.

(Silence.)

TEENAGE SUTTER

There are no trees out back and the dog died last year.

MIDDLE-AGED MOTHER

Are you giving us word for word?

TEENAGE SUTTER

I don't understand what any of this has to do with what I just said.

MIDDLE-AGED MOTHER

What about it don't you understand?

TEENAGE SUTTER

A man followed me home. And you're asking me what did I do??? You're telling me to start wrestling and stop doing musicals and—

MIDDLE-AGED MOTHER

What is that book you're reading?

(She takes the book.)

TEENAGE SUTTER

. . . Jackie Collins' new book.

MIDDLE-AGED MOTHER

Where did you get THIS?

TEENAGE SUTTER

The library.

MIDDLE-AGED MOTHER

Don't this book got a lot of fuckin in it.

TEENAGE SUTTER

(Duh) It's Jackie Collins.

MIDDLE-AGED MOTHER

(Flipping pages) Barbara has been sitting up there at that front desk all damn week reading this same damn book, I knew it looked similah. She been sittin up there talking about it on that damn phone and all I could hear coming out her damn mouth was about how somebody fucked somebody else. From what Barbara be talking this book is ALL about nuthin but fuckin. And you mean to tell me that you have been sitting here night after night at my dinner table reading books about fuckin!

TEENAGE SUTTER

I read Stephen King too.

STEPFATHER

Ain't his books about killing folks?

TEENAGE SUTTER

Not exactly—

MIDDLE-AGED MOTHER

Have you lost your mind in real life?

TEENAGE SUTTER

No ma'am.

MIDDLE-AGED MOTHER

I go to work every day to put clothes on your back and Happy Meals in your mouth and you come to this table reading books about killing and fuckin . . . THAT'S why that damn man from Iran was following you home. If every time he sees you, you sitting up somewhere reading about killing and fuckin it must mean you want to be kilt and then fucked.

(Silence.)

TEENAGE SUTTER

I finished all the *Encyclopedia Brown*s that they have in the library so I just started reading—

MIDDLE-AGED MOTHER

Encyclopedia who???

TEENAGE SUTTER

Brown.

MIDDLE-AGED MOTHER

What Brown got to do with it? I'm sitting here trying to figure out how to stop you from being raped up the ass and you talking about colors . . . You need to Grow. Up . . . You are getting too old to be sitting up in here reading all damn day.

STEPFATHER

Calm down honey.

MIDDLE-AGED MOTHER

No. This is a conversation that needs to be had and if you're not going to have it, cuz you ain't his real damn daddy, then I guess I will have to have it.

(To Teenage Sutter) I knew there was going to be troubles with you. Your grandmama told me that I shouldn't be making you wash dishes and do laundry but I told her to mind her own damn bizness cuz you was my chile. But I knew from the moment you walked in here when you was little asking me about periods and blowjobs that you was going to bring me the troubles. You the only little boy that would come asking his

mama why his dick was crooked and why his pee came out to the left side.

STEPFATHER

It's okay, honey.

MIDDLE-AGED MOTHER

Bootycandies! That's what he was concerned about when he was little and now I see that I should have never given you that damn dictionary because now all you is interested in is reading some ol nasty shit. How on earth do you expect to get a woman when you grow up if all you know how to do is read . . . and clap . . . and do musicals? . . . You will NOT be going to show choir camp THIS summer you can forget about that!

TEENAGE SUTTER

But Mom!!!

MIDDLE-AGED MOTHER

Don't But Mom Me! This summer you will learn to CATCH. SOMETHIN! . . . I don't give a damn what kind of ball it is but you will spend this coming summer with BALLS in yo FACE!!!

(Silence.)

Period.

*(She gets up from the table and leaves, taking the Jackie Collins book.
Silence.*
Stepfather sits for an awkward moment. He tries to say something but he is just . . . awkward.
He gets up and leaves.
Teenage Sutter looks over at Young Sibling who has been sitting playing with a Happy Meal toy this entire time.
Silence.)

TEENAGE SUTTER

(Quiet) Call . . . Granny.

YOUNG SIBLING

For what?

TEENAGE SUTTER

Ask her if we can come over this weekend.

YOUNG SIBLING

Why caint you axe her yourself?

TEENAGE SUTTER

I'm too old to be asking if I can come over.

(Beat.)

YOUNG SIBLING

What the fuck do I get if I axe her.

TEENAGE SUTTER

. . . I'll teach you that new dance Michael Jackson do.

YOUNG SIBLING

. . . Promise.

TEENAGE SUTTER

Promise.

(Beat.
    Young Sibling gets up and leaves with the toys.
    Silence.
    Teenage Sutter sits a moment.
    Then.
    He reaches under the table and retrieves a Stephen King paperback.
    He opens his book and reads.)

SCENE 8

Ceremony

An Officiant stands in front of an audience at this ceremony.

OFFICIANT

Dearly beloved. Today is the beginning of a bold new step to clarity and fulfillment. You have been asked here to bear witness. Witness to a profound and sacred ceremony that stands in the face of homophobia and all prejudice. Witness to two individuals who not just five years ago requested your presence in this exact same tropical destination for what they believed then would be an everlasting celebration of their love and . . . commitment. You come here today to share a moment of non-commitment. Therefore, on behalf of Genitalia and Intifada. Welcome.

(Two obvious lesbians enter.)

Today we come to encourage, celebrate and support the covenant these two people, Genitalia and Intifada, beloved to us, now make, and to share in the joy that Genitalia and Intifada are feeling as they pledge their non-commitment to each other. We rejoice and celebrate in the ways life has led them to each other and got them to the place where they now stand.

(To Genitalia) Genitalia, the woman who stands here is going to be your ex-partner. She will no longer look to you for comfort, for support, for love, for understanding, for encouragement, nor for protection. You may now take her for granted, and never have to stand by her for good or ill.

GENITALIA

(To Intifada) Intifada . . . Today. In the presence of God and family and friends, I sever my life from yours. Wherever you go, I will not be there. Whatever you face, you will face without me.

OFFICIANT

Intifada. What I said to her. Consider me having said it to you.

INTIFADA

(To Genitalia) Genitalia, what you have said to me, I now say back to you and would like to add that you Fuck Yourself.

OFFICIANT

And now a passage will be read by Reverend Benson.

(Reverend Benson appears.)

REVEREND BENSON

In the Bible, Cicely Tyson wrote so beautifully about the power of hatred in her First Book of Letters to the Hobbits:

"Get your own milk and sugar, muthafucka"

"I speak in tongues of men and devils, but have not love, I am nosy and vindictive and funky."

"And if I have prophetic powers, and understand all mysteries and all knowledge, and if I have all faith, so as to remove the mountains of bullshit, but have not love, then fuck it, I will have not love."

"Hatred bears all things, believes all things, hopes all things, endures all things."

"When I was a child, I spoke like child, I thought like a child, I reasoned like a child, when I became a man, I went on the internet, and spoke like a child, and thought like a child, and reasoned like child."

"So faith, hope, hatred abide, these three; but the greatest of these is hatred"

"Get your own milk and sugar . . . muthafucka."

(Reverend Benson exits.

Beat.

Genitalia takes out a piece of folded colorful paper and begins to read.)

GENITALIA

"I Genitalia, named so by my mother, Adella Missatoof, a trail-blazer before her time, who decided that her daughter should know that with a beautiful name comes many haters. I, affirm my hatred for you, Intifada, as I invite you to die a slow painful death from this very moment. You are the most ugly, stupid, self-centered person I have ever known. With unkindness, selfishness, and cynicism, I will work against your side to create a living hell for you. I evict you, Intifada, from my condo, to no longer have and no longer hold, from this day forward, for my better and your worse, for my richer and your poorer, in your sickness and my health, for as long as I shall live and you shall suffer."

(Intifada takes out a piece of folded colorful paper and begins to read.)

INTIFADA

"Genitalia, your mama was a fool and a ho. Your name attached to your face, means Stank Pussy. And I, Intifada, from the moment I first saw you, knew you were the one who would steal my money. Your cancerous heart, and your brain tumor inspired me to treat you like the cunt you revealed yourself to be. I promise to hate you for eternity, disrespecting you, dishonoring you, being as unfaithful to you now as I have been throughout our whole disgusting relationship. This is my solemn vowel."

(Silence.

Genitalia takes out another piece of folded colorful paper and begins to read.)

GENITALIA

"Intifada, today I become your Ex and you become my Ex-Lax. I shit you out of my life. I promise to keep myself closed off from you, and never again let you into my innermost fears or feelings, secrets or dreams. I promise to grow old without you, to be unwilling to face change as we both change, keeping our relationship dead and cold."

(Silence.

Intifada takes out another piece of colorful folded paper and begins to read.)

INTIFADA

"Genitalia, today I become your Ex-Lax . . . And hope you are constipated."

OFFICIANT

Since it is your intention to be non-committed, join your fists and declare your consent.

(Genitalia and Intifada fist bump.)

OFFICIANT

Genitalia, do you take Intifada to be your unlawfully non-committed ex as long as you both shall live.

GENITALIA

I do.

OFFICIANT

Intifada, do you take Genitalia for the unlawfully non-committed ex stuff I just said?

INTIFADA

I don't.

(Silence.)

OFFICIANT

Excuse me?

INTIFADA

(To Genitalia) I love you . . . let's work it out . . . I need you . . .

GENITALIA

Intifada—

INTIFADA

Genitalia, I love you. I want to grow old with you. Let's give us another chance. Please.

(Silence.
    Genitalia looks to the gathered audience.
    Then back to Intifada.)

Please baby.

GENITALIA

. . . Okay.

INTIFADA

Sike!! You stupid DYKE. I hate your fucking guts and don't want to see you again until they're carving up your fucking tumor for science.

(To Officiant) My answer is I do.

OFFICIANT

The ceremonial rings symbolize unity, a circle unbroken, without beginning or end. And today, Genitalia and Intifada take back their rings, as a confirmation of their vows to non-commit, to work at all times to create a life that is incomplete and broken, to never love each other again. May the Lord bless these rings which you take from each other as a symbol of your hatred and infidelity.

(To Genitalia) Take her hand, and state your pledge to her, repeating after me.

(Genitalia takes Intifada's hand in her own.)

With this ring I non-commit.

GENITALIA

With this ring I non-commit.

OFFICIANT

I remove my hand and heart as I know they will be unsafe with you.

GENITALIA

I remove my hand and heart as I know they will be unsafe with you.

OFFICIANT

All that I am I sever from you and that I have I remove from you.

GENITALIA

All that I am I sever from you and that I have I remove from you.

(Genitalia removes the ring from Intifada's finger.
  Intifada takes Genitalia hand in hers.)

INTIFADA

With this ring I non-commit. I remove my hand and heart as I know they will be unsafe with you. All that I am I sever from you and I have I remove from you.

(Intifada removes the ring from Genitalia's finger.)

OFFICIANT

Genitalia and Intifada, you have given and pledged your promises to each other, and declared your everlasting hatred by removing the rings. Your vows may have been spoken in minutes, but your promises to each other will last until your last breath. Genitalia and Intifada, you have pledged to meet sorrow and happiness as two separate families before God and this community of friends.

(Silence. Genitalia and Intifada take in the gravity it all.)

I now pronounce you Ex and Ex-Lax. You may now bitch slap each other.

(They proceed to bitch slap each other.)

SCENE 9

The Last Gay Play

Sutter and Larry, sit at a table sipping cocktails, kee-keeing.
A New York Times *is on the table between them.*
Clint sits at a table next to them, also having a drink.

LARRY

So what happened?

SUTTER

After I spoke to you?

LARRY

No after you spoke to the pope—of course after you spoke to
me—what happened?

SUTTER

(Coy) Well, he came over.

LARRY

Wait—go back.

SUTTER

What?

LARRY

Go to the part where you met him.

SUTTER

I told you he answered my ad—

LARRY

You have an ad?

SUTTER

Yeah. So do you.

(Silence.)

LARRY

First of all. I never invite TRADE immediately over to my house. First we meet. Somewhere in public—

SUTTER

So an-ti-way! He came over—

(Clint turns to Larry and Sutter.)

CLINT

I'm sorry I was just wondering . . .
　(He turns to Sutter) Your voice is weird. It's rather . . . feminine.

SUTTER

Excuse me?

CLINT

Are you gay?

SUTTER

No . . .
(À la Grey Poupon commercial) But I do have a taste for dick
every now and then.

(Silence.
  Larry tries not to laugh.)

CLINT

So you're gay?

SUTTER

We're having a conversation here, I don't think—

CLINT

Would you mind if I joined you?

SUTTER

Are you drunk?

CLINT

Yeah.

(Sutter looks to Larry.
  Larry makes a slight negative gesture.
  Sutter smiles.)

SUTTER

You can join us. But you have to play nice. No rude comments
or I'm going to have to ask you to leave.

CLINT

Fine.

(Clint pulls his chair up to Larry and Sutter's table.)

I'm Clint.

LARRY

Larry.

SUTTER

Sutter.

CLINT

Do you guys wanna buy me a drink.

SUTTER

No.

CLINT

Okay. I'll be back.

(Clint exits off to the bar.)

LARRY

What are you doing?

SUTTER

I'm gonna have a little fun.

LARRY

I don't think we should.

SUTTER

He interrupted our conversation he was rude and I want to play with him for a bit.

LARRY

I just don't think this is going to turn out—

SUTTER

I'm not gonna attack the guy.

LARRY

Okay fine, but if it gets outta hand, I'm leaving.

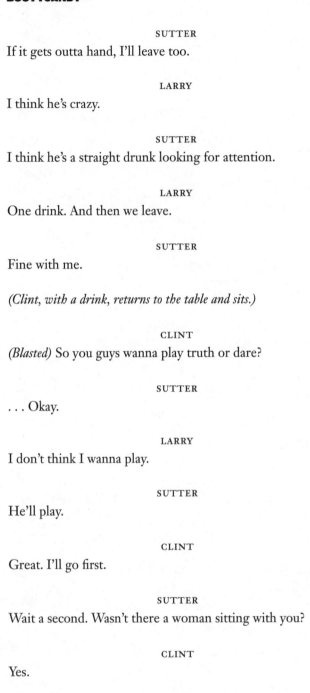

SUTTER

If it gets outta hand, I'll leave too.

LARRY

I think he's crazy.

SUTTER

I think he's a straight drunk looking for attention.

LARRY

One drink. And then we leave.

SUTTER

Fine with me.

(Clint, with a drink, returns to the table and sits.)

CLINT

(Blasted) So you guys wanna play truth or dare?

SUTTER

. . . Okay.

LARRY

I don't think I wanna play.

SUTTER

He'll play.

CLINT

Great. I'll go first.

SUTTER

Wait a second. Wasn't there a woman sitting with you?

CLINT

Yes.

SUTTER

Is she your girlfriend?

CLINT

No. I met her online.

(Sutter and Larry exchange looks.)

SUTTER

Why did she leave?

CLINT

I told her I wanted to fuck her. Truth or dare?

SUTTER

Truth.

CLINT

What was the last thing you had up your ass?

SUTTER

A cock.

CLINT

Not a dildo?

SUTTER

No.

CLINT

Not a finger?

SUTTER

No.

CLINT

How big was the cock?

>   SUTTER

Isn't it my turn?

>   CLINT

Okay.

>   SUTTER

(To Clint) Truth or dare.

>   CLINT

DARE.

>   SUTTER

Pull your dick out and put it on the table right now.

(Without a moment's hesitation, Clint stands and pulls his cock out and places it on the table in front of Sutter and Larry.)

>   LARRY

(Quick) I'm leaving.

>   SUTTER

Wait.

>   LARRY

I'm going.

>   CLINT

(Putting his cock back in his pants) Truth or dare.

>   SUTTER

(To Larry) Don't go.

>   LARRY

Don't dare him again.

>   CLINT

Truth or dare.

SUTTER

Truth.

CLINT

What is the biggest dick you've had in your ass?

SUTTER

I don't know. Truth or dare.

CLINT

Dare.

LARRY

Don't.

CLINT

Dare.

LARRY

Do. Not.

SUTTER

(Excited) Kiss my friend Larry.

(Clint kisses Larry.
Larry is stunned.)

CLINT

(To Larry) Truth or dare.

LARRY

. . .

SUTTER

Larry.

LARRY

. . . Truth.

> CLINT

How big is your dick?

> LARRY

Nine inches.

> SUTTER

What!!

> LARRY

(Nonchalant) My girlfriend in high school measured it once.

> CLINT

You had a girlfriend?

> LARRY

Long time ago.

> SUTTER

You have a nine-inch cock??

> LARRY

Yes.
    (To Clint) Truth or dare.

> CLINT

Truth.

> LARRY

Thank God. Okay. Um . . . Have you ever had sex with a guy?

> CLINT

Yes. Truth or dare.

> SUTTER

I still can't believe you have a nine-inch cock.

LARRY

Get over it.

CLINT

Truth or dare.

SUTTER

Truth.

CLINT

You guys wanna come back to my hotel?

(Black.
    Then light.
    Larry and Sutter sit at the table. They have had several additional drinks. Clint is not there.)

LARRY

Do you have any idea what time it is?

SUTTER

When are we going to have another opportunity like this one?

LARRY

Sutter, the guy is around the corner buying extra-large condoms.

SUTTER

I don't think he'll come back.

LARRY

He took his dick out and placed it on our table, he'll come back!

SUTTER

I think he's lying.

LARRY

I'm not FUCKING HIM!

SUTTER

Larry calm down, we won't even get that far. We'll walk him to his hotel . . . IF he's actually staying in a hotel which I doubt. And we'll see what type of excuses he makes up to get out of it.

LARRY

What if he doesn't make up an excuse!

SUTTER

What's the worse thing that could happen? We'll get to his hotel, he'll make an excuse OR he'll call OUR bluff.

LARRY

That's cruel.

SUTTER

What's cruel about it? He's the one that asked us back to his hotel. You act like he's a fourteen-year-old girl. He's a grown man.

LARRY

It's still cruel.

SUTTER

Fuck that.

LARRY

Sutter.

SUTTER

(Serious) Fuck that Larry, I want to humiliate him.

LARRY

. . . Why?

SUTTER

(Deadly) Because I can.

LARRY

What are you talking about?

SUTTER

You know what I'm talking about . . . Just for the fun of it.

LARRY

For the fun of what?

SUTTER

He's drunk.

LARRY

You're drunk.

SUTTER

He's corny and horny. He's staying at a Best Western. In Brooklyn. It's perfect.

LARRY

What are you saying?

SUTTER

You know what I'm saying. You knew what I was saying when I began to say it so stop asking me "what am I saying" instead ask yourself why the fuck are you still here?

(Silence.)

(Whispering) I can't do this by myself.

LARRY

I'm not—

SUTTER

You just have to hold him down. I'll do the rest.

(Silence.
  Clint returns with condoms and beer. He's sloppy now.
  Larry turns to Clint.)

LARRY

Why do you want to do this?

CLINT

It'll be fun.

LARRY

You're not gay?

CLINT

Nope.

LARRY

But you want to get fucked?

CLINT

Yep.

LARRY

Why?

CLINT

Because I want to be humiliated.

(Larry turns to Sutter.
  Sutter smiles.
  Black.
  Then light.
  Larry, Sutter and Clint at the hotel.
  Clint holds a key card in his hands.)

(Pausing) . . . Wait.

SUTTER

I knew you were bullshit.

CLINT

You have to give me a moment to clean up my room. I haven't had maid service for about two weeks.

LARRY

How long have you been here?

CLINT

Two weeks.

(Beat.)

SUTTER

I want to see what it looks like . . . Before you clean it up.

LARRY

Why?

CLINT

Why?

SUTTER

Because I think you're bullshit.

CLINT

Okay.

(Clint swipes his card.
The sound of a door opening is heard.)

> SUTTER

(Astonished) Okay. We'll wait out here.

(Clint exits.
  Lights shift.)

> LARRY

(Quiet) What the fuck?

> SUTTER

(Quiet) That was disgusting.

> LARRY

I told you he was crazy.

> SUTTER

He is demented.

> LARRY

There was shit and blood on that towel on the floor.

> SUTTER

You saw shit?

> LARRY

And blood. I'm not kidding.

> SUTTER

Did you see the peanut butter jar?

> LARRY

With the MetroCard in it?

> SUTTER

He's been using a MetroCard to eat peanut butter.

LARRY

And the dildos?

SUTTER

That big black one?

LARRY

Yeah. And the BED!

SUTTER

Shhhhh someone might hear us.

LARRY

We should leave.

(Clint enters completely naked except for a hotel blanket draped on his shoulders.
    Silence.)

CLINT

What's wrong? . . . You guys don't want to do it anymore? If you guys didn't want to do it then why did you guys come back here?

LARRY

You know what? We're really sorry but we can't do this.

CLINT

(Broken) Then why did you come? Why didn't you just say no and tell me to get lost?

LARRY

We thought you were kidding.

CLINT

After I put my dick on the table you thought I was kidding?

(Beat.)

SUTTER

. . . Yes.

CLINT

You know how embarrassing this is for me? I went online to try to meet someone . . . Just to have a good time. She didn't want to have anything to do with me when I said what I honestly felt.

SUTTER

Clint—

CLINT

I just wanted to have fun with you guys!!

(Silence.)

SUTTER

We're sorry.

CLINT

That's not good enough!! I'm not some fucking toy you can play around with and lead on and then decide you don't— I have feelings you know. I'm standing here naked in front of two strangers hoping to have a little experience—

SUTTER

We didn't think—

CLINT

I just want to get FUCKED!

(Silence.)

I just want to be held. And fucked.

(Silence.)

SUTTER

Clint . . . Can I ask you a serious question.

CLINT

Will you hold me?

SUTTER

Clint.

CLINT

Please. I just want to feel human. Contact. Just for a moment. Touch me.

(Sutter looks to Larry.
Larry nods to Sutter to go to Clint.
Clint slowly approaches Sutter, who takes him in his arms.)

(Honest) I repulse a lot of people I know that. I drink too much I laugh too loud I smell funny my eyes are too far apart I'm pigeon-toed. And I have nasty thoughts . . .

SUTTER

(Quiet) Clint. Are you on any medication.

CLINT

They make me sleep . . .

LARRY

Maybe you should take them . . . Until you . . . Get to a better place . . .

CLINT

I don't want to leave my room. Don't wanna go to work. Sometimes I don't even feel like getting up and going to the bath-

room . . . I like pain sometimes . . . That's why . . . that's why
I asked you guys back here . . . for some pleasure . . . pain.

(Silence.
Black.
Then light.
Larry and Sutter sit having drinks.
Larry reads the New York Times *that has been sitting at the*
table throughout.)

SUTTER

(Referring to the Times*)* I don't think that was him.

LARRY

It was him. I can't believe we did that.

SUTTER

He wanted us to—

LARRY

We did it.

SUTTER

We didn't do anything. Nothing was done.

LARRY

What about the desk clerk at the Best Western?

SUTTER

There wasn't a desk clerk at the Best Western.

LARRY

He was sleeping.

SUTTER

There wasn't a desk clerk. It was four A.M. Clint had a key card
for the front door and to his hotel room.

LARRY

When we were leaving—

SUTTER

What?

LARRY

When we were leaving there was a desk clerk sleeping . . .

SUTTER

There wasn't a fucking—

LARRY

I think he smiled at me . . .

SUTTER

I thought you said he was sleeping.

LARRY

I think he might have smiled at me though. Like he knew we had just come from having a good time with one of the guests.

SUTTER

So what.

LARRY

They're going to catch us.

SUTTER

No they are not.

LARRY

Every place has cameras.

SUTTER

Listen to me—

LARRY

And we're back at the same fucking place where we met him. This was a stupid idea . . .

SUTTER

This was the ONLY idea . . . We don't change our routine. You know how many fucking guys come to this city every day and go to bars every night and go back to their fucking hotel rooms with strangers . . .

LARRY

No I don't know, how many Sutter??

SUTTER

Lots!

(Silence.)

LARRY

I don't know who you are anymore.

SUTTER

I'm the guy who watched you hold a man down while we raped him with a big black dildo. Remember me now?

(Silence.)

LARRY

I could go to them and tell them it was your idea.

SUTTER

I'm smaller and younger than you.

LARRY

He killed himself because of what we did to him.

SUTTER

No, he walked up to that roof and jumped into traffic because he was off his medicine.

LARRY

A guy died. We had something to do with it and you feel no fucking REMORSE!

SUTTER

Did we beat him with bricks? Did we impale him on a fucking fence??! Did we attach him to our fucking car and drag him through the fucking streets? Did we?! You think those fuckers feel any remorse—

LARRY

I don't want to become them.

SUTTER

It felt good didn't it? To get back at one of them. It felt good.

LARRY

No.

SUTTER

Truth or dare.

LARRY

Fuck you.

SUTTER

Truth or dare.

LARRY

. . .

> SUTTER

TRUTH or—

> LARRY

Dare!

(Silence.
They look to each other.)

> SUTTER

I dare you to go to the police right now and tell them everything.

(Silence.
Larry starts to leave. Then comes back.)

> LARRY

(Suffering) This will haunt me for the rest of my life.

> SUTTER

I'm sorry—

> LARRY

Don't call me ever again. Don't write me another email or text or speak to me even if you see me begging in the fucking streets.

> SUTTER

We didn't kill him Larry.

> LARRY

Truth or dare.

> SUTTER

Truth.

(Silence.)

LARRY

You've done this before . . .

(Sutter looks at him.
Larry exits.
Sutter sits.
Silence.
Actor 4/Larry reenters abruptly and out of character. He adlibs his frustration over the scene and it brings the other actors to the stage from various entrances.
They are dressed in correctional outfits.)

ACTOR 5

I don't understand this uh—you have in the scene Sutter holding Clint in his arms, rubbing him like a baby and then they take him into the room and rape him? . . .

SUTTER

I'm not quite sure about that.

ACTOR 4

The scene goes too far. It's false and gratuitous.

ACTOR 1

It feels like you want to play the victim.

SUTTER

Excuse me.

ACTOR 4

We've been investing in this because we were under the impression that this was based on real events . . .

SUTTER

It's not.

ACTOR

So what is the fucking audience suppose to think??

SUTTER

I don't wanna do your acting . . . job . . . for you.

(*The actors look to each other.*)

ACTOR 1

(*British accent*) Why did you hire us?

ACTOR 3

(*British accent*) Do you think we're black?

SUTTER

You . . . You are black.

ACTOR 1

(*British accent*) We're putting on those accents you understand . . .

ACTOR 3

(*British accent*) We're not Negroes.

ACTOR 4

(*Offended*) What???

ACTOR 1

(*British accent*) We're English.

SUTTER

. . . I think you should just—

ACTOR 5

You are truly fucked-up, and just because some man followed
you home from the library and eventually fucked you when you

were sixteen, and you've experienced unrequited love, doesn't mean that you need to rape a mentally unstable person with a big black dildo . . . And kill him.

ACTOR 1

This has all been some sick fantasy of yours.

ACTOR 3

So why do you need ACTORS???

ACTORS

Exactly!!!

(Silence.
Sutter looks to the Actual Stage Manager's booth.)

SUTTER

I'm sorry I'm uh um I'm sorry [stage manager's name]. Could we um . . .

ACTUAL STAGE MANAGER

Hold please.

(Sutter is silent. He looks at the audience. He becomes emotional . . .
he stifles himself.
The actors break character further and become their real selves . . .
Eventually the actor playing Sutter looks back up at the Actual
Stage Manager's booth.)

SUTTER

I need my grandmother.

(Silence. The actors look to Sutter.)

(Quietly to Actor 4) Could I have my grandmother please.

(Beat.)

ACTUAL STAGE MANAGER

Okay everyone we're going to skip the Prison. And go directly into iPhone.

(The stage becomes a machine as we hear the Actual Stage Manager calling for the requirements of the scene change.

Everyone involved in the production of this play begins to set the next scene.

Sets, lights, costumes.

Everything needed for the next scene is done right in front of the audience.

We hear the Actual Stage Manager calling the cues to get us into the next scene ending with:)

. . . . Go.

SCENE 10

iPhone

A nursing home.

An Old Granny sits in a wheelchair watching Judge Judy *or soaps or the like.*

She can't move her left arm or right leg because of a stroke.

Her adult grandson, Sutter, is there.

SUTTER

Hi Granny.

(Old Granny looks away.)

. . . What's wrong Granny?

OLD GRANNY

Who you?

SUTTER

. . . You don't recognize me Granny?

(Old Granny looks at him and then away again.)

OLD GRANNY

Who you?

SUTTER

I'm your grandson, Granny. Sutter Boy.

OLD GRANNY

. . . I don't know you.

(Sutter takes out twenty dollars and holds it out to Granny.)

SUTTER

Here Granny.

(Old Granny turns and sees the twenty-dollar bill.)

OLD GRANNY

(Reaching for the bill with her good arm) Hey baby, how you doin?

SUTTER

I'm doing alright. How you doing?

OLD GRANNY

These folks in here don't wanna feed nobody nothing.

SUTTER

They haven't been feeding you?

OLD GRANNY

Nawl, they take some gatdamn cord and put in my belly and tell me that that's feeding me. How you gone feed me with a cord in my belly. I need food in my mouth.

SUTTER

Mama said that the doctor told you you can't eat solid food anymore. You been having a hard time swallowing.

OLD GRANNY

Fuck that doctor. I wants me some ribs and some gatdamn macaroni and cheese and some—

SUTTER

Granny you can't have any of that anymore.

OLD GRANNY

Why not?

SUTTER

Because Mama said the doctor said—

OLD GRANNY

Yo mama don't know what the fuck she talkin about that gatdamn doctor ain't say no kinda shit like that.

SUTTER

Well you can't have ribs. You might choke to death.

OLD GRANNY

I been eating ribs fo goin on eighty-five gatdamn years and I ain't choked to death on nothin why all of sudden I can't have no food in my mouth? How much sense that make?

SUTTER

I know.

OLD GRANNY

Run down there and pick me up some of em baby backs.

> SUTTER

Granny. That's not going to happen.

(Silence.
  Old Granny looks away.)

> OLD GRANNY

Who you?

> SUTTER

Oh now we're back to Alzheimer's? After you done took my twenty dollars.

> OLD GRANNY

It was suppose to be a FIFTY.

> SUTTER

What you gone do with fifty dollars in a nursing home?

> OLD GRANNY

Whatever the fuck I like.

> SUTTER

You wanna lose it on Bingo Thursdays?

> OLD GRANNY

I ain't never lost no gatdamn fifty dollars at no bingo been goin to bingo for near bout sixty-five years and I ain't never lost no gatdamn FIFTY.

> SUTTER

I brought you something.

> OLD GRANNY

Ribs?

SUTTER

No not ribs Granny. Memories.

OLD GRANNY

Do them memories come with barbecue sauce on em? If not, "Who you?"

(Silence.
   Sutter takes out an iPhone.)

What that do?

SUTTER

Lots. You remember how I use to record you and Granddaddy cussin and fussin all the time.

OLD GRANNY

I don't fuckin cuss.

(Silence.)

SUTTER

I thought I lost all those old tapes . . . I use to record you all the time. Especially when you were yellin at me about something. I put them in storage a while ago and forgot about them . . . but then . . . I realized . . . I could get them digitized . . . took me a few months but . . . Listen.

(He pushes his iPhone.
   Lights shift on Old Granny.)

OLD GRANNY

"You laugh like a grown gross gray ass frog."

(He pushes.)

"Your voice rings all through me like a bell clapper on a goose's ass"

(He pushes.)

"Sit yo ass down and stop skippin cross this gatdamn flo. Don't you hear that gatdamn thunder and lightin??!!!"

(Lights shift back.)

Where the hell did you get those from?

SUTTER

I told you I recorded them when I was little.

OLD GRANNY

Why on earth would you ever record some shit like that?

SUTTER

Because I loved the way you spoke.

OLD GRANNY

The way I spoke? I spoke like a human person.

SUTTER

No Granny. You spoke a little different.

OLD GRANNY

I spoke like everybody else spoke—

(He pushes the iPhone again.
Lights shift.)

"I can't even wipe my ass without somebody callin my GAT-damn name!"

(Lights shift back.)

SUTTER

I got conversations. Like you and Mama.

(He pushes.
Lights shift.
Middle-Aged Mother appears in a wedding dress.)

OLD GRANNY

(To Middle-Aged Mother) What the fuck you gon put on a white dress fo?

MIDDLE-AGED MOTHER

What's wrong with this white dress?

OLD GRANNY

What's wrong with it?

MIDDLE-AGED MOTHER

Yeah what's wrong with it Mama?

OLD GRANNY

Ask them two gatdamn kids you already gat from two different baby daddies what's wrong with it?

MIDDLE-AGED MOTHER

That don't mean nothing. That's old-fashion to think you can't wear a white dress just because you have kids.

OLD GRANNY

By two different baby daddies.

MIDDLE-AGED MOTHER

You had twelve gatdamn kids Mama!

OLD GRANNY

And they all gat the SAME GATdamn BABY DADDY.

MIDDLE-AGED MOTHER

Well I'm wearing this WHITE dress at my wedding.

OLD GRANNY

Then I won't be there.

MIDDLE-AGED MOTHER

What?

OLD GRANNY

And you can't have it in my gatdamn church with my gatdamn pastor.

MIDDLE-AGED MOTHER

You don't run that church.

OLD GRANNY

You ain't gon be struttin down no gatdamn aisle of MY church in a white gatdamn dress with two gatdamn kids from two different baby daddies carryin rings behind you.

MIDDLE-AGED MOTHER

This is my wedding day Mama. Not yours!

(Middle-Aged Mother stomps out.
    Lights shift back.)

SUTTER

Mama cried all that night.

OLD GRANNY

She got married tho didn't she?

SUTTER

Yes ma'am.

OLD GRANNY

In my church?

SUTTER

Yes ma'am.

OLD GRANNY

Was I there?

SUTTER

Yes you were there Granny.

OLD GRANNY

Is she happy?

(Silence.)

SUTTER

Yes. I think she's happy Granny.

OLD GRANNY

Then that's all that matters.

(Silence.
He drops the iPhone by mistake.
Lights shift.
A White Man appears.)

May I help you sir?

WHITE MAN

Yes I'm looking for a young man, named Sutter.

OLD GRANNY

That's my grandson, how may I help you sir?

WHITE MAN

He's friends with my son, Roy.

OLD GRANNY

Okay.

WHITE MAN

I saw Sutter the other day and I just wanted to make sure he was alright.

OLD GRANNY

Is somethin the matter sir.

WHITE MAN

No ma'am. I just wanted to make sure that . . . that he was okay.

OLD GRANNY

Why wouldn't he be okay?
    (To offstage) Sutter Boy!!

(Sutter speaks in the opposite direction of Old Granny.)

SUTTER

(Laughing to offstage) Ma'am??

OLD GRANNY

(To offstage) Come out heah!

(Sutter becomes a teenager . . .)

SUTTER

(Still laughing to Old Granny) Ma'am?

(Sutter notices the White Man.
    They stare at each other for long moment.
    A secret is shared between them.)

OLD GRANNY

You know this man, Sutter Boy?

SUTTER

Yes ma'am.

OLD GRANNY

Somethin happen that he need to be comin here to make sure
you alright?

SUTTER

Yes ma'am.

OLD GRANNY

. . . Is you alright?

SUTTER

. . . I'm alright.

*(Old Granny looks to White Man who has not stopped looking at
Sutter.)*

WHITE MAN

. . . Good . . .

OLD GRANNY

How do you know my Sutter Boy, sir?

WHITE MAN

Oh . . . we met at the library.

(Beat.)

And he knows my son, Roy.

(Silence.
White Man disappears.
Lights shift back.)

OLD GRANNY

Is that suppose to mean somethin to me?

SUTTER

. . . No ma'am . . . It means something to me . . . I must have left the tape recorder on . . . sometimes I'd hide it in the hallway . . . then listen to what it recorded later at night . . .

OLD GRANNY

There is really somethin wrong with you boy.

SUTTER

That's not the one I wanted you to hear. This is the one.

OLD GRANNY

Is you gonna run on down there and—

(He pushes the iPhone.
Lights shift.
Young Black Mom appears.
Sutter is now young.)

Do that move Michael Jackson lak ta do.

(Sutter does some old-school MJ moves.
Young Black Mom watches.)

(Clapping) Get it . . . Get it . . . Get it . . . Get it . . .

YOUNG BLACK MOM

That's all he like to do. Dance and read that dictionary I bought him.

OLD GRANNY

Ain't nuthin wrong with dat . . . You wait till he start runnin behind these little girls you better hope he just want to dance and read some dictionary book stead of gettin one of em fast-tail heifas pregnant . . .

YOUNG BLACK MOM

I ain't raisin nobody's babies.

OLD GRANNY

That's exactly what I said before you had this one and look how many times you dropping him off over here for the weekENDS that turns into the week BEGINS.

YOUNG BLACK MOM

I need a break sometimes.

OLD GRANNY

And I don't need no gatdamn break?? I was just suppose to raise my twelve gatdamn kids and THEY kids too???? . . .

YOUNG BLACK MOM

Mama you know you like to have them runnin all over the place.

OLD GRANNY

What the hell makes you think that?

YOUNG BLACK MOM

Cuz you let em.

>   OLD GRANNY

I let em cuz I don't want them out there in them streets like you and yo gatdamn hardheaded brothers and sisters . . . all yall know how to do was eat, shit and run the streets.

(Sutter stops doing MJ moves and catches his breath but speaks anyway.)

>   SUTTER

Granny—

>   YOUNG BLACK MOM

Don't you hear me and Mama talkin? I don told you about interruptin grown people's conversation.

>   SUTTER

But I got a question about my bootycandy.

>   OLD GRANNY

What???

>   YOUNG BLACK MOM

(To Sutter) Shut up and go sit down somewhere.

>   OLD GRANNY

Wait a second—

>   YOUNG BLACK MOM

Mama don't—

>   OLD GRANNY

What he wanna know about a bootycandy fo?

>   YOUNG BLACK MOM

I don't know what he wanna know he been talkin about it for the last week, he got some letter from that little mannish girl, Alessa, next door to me, need her ass beat.

OLD GRANNY

What you wanna know about bootycandies fo Sutter?

YOUNG BLACK MOM

Mama I said—

OLD GRANNY

You member to pull yourself back and wash?

YOUNG BLACK MOM

Gatdammit. Here we go.

SUTTER

I always remember to pull myself back and wash, but Granny, Mama said if I forget to do it, then my bootycandy would fall off.

(Silence.
Old Granny looks to Young Black Mom.)

OLD GRANNY

You told this boy his dick would fall off?

SUTTER

Mama say you ain't suppose to say "dick," Granny.

OLD GRANNY

That's a damn shame.
(To Sutter) Your bootycandy will not fall off.

SUTTER

That's what I thought. Mama said you ain't suppose to lick it or let nobody else lick it.

(Old Granny looks to Young Black Mom.)

YOUNG BLACK MOM

You started it. Gone finish it.

OLD GRANNY

(*To Sutter*) You ain't suppose to lick it Sutter. But . . . When you get older . . . Some folks lak to have it licked . . .

SUTTER

Like them folks in them magazines that Uncle Terry and Uncle Alphonso have under the bathtub upstairs?

(*Silence.*
Old Granny looks to Young Black Mom, who smiles broadly.)

YOUNG BLACK MOM

(*To Old Granny; mocking*) "Get it . . . Get it . . . Get it . . ."

(*Young Black Mom disappears.*)

SUTTER

Why them bootycandies so BIG!! Is that what happens when they get happy from the lickin!!??? And Granny, I got a idea about somethin . . . I think that if boys was just allowed to lick other boys' bootycandies, there would be peace in the world cuz then they wouldn't be mad at each other and start tryin to kill each other cuz they bootycandies would be happy and they would grow big from the lickin and they could play bootycandy games instead of making wars and stuff.

(*Dead silence.*
Lights shift back.)

OLD GRANNY

You have lost your mind in real life.

(Silence.)

SUTTER

When was the last time you had ribs Granny? . . .

OLD GRANNY

I can't remember, why?

SUTTER

You really want some?

OLD GRANNY

No. I really want some mo of that tofu pumped into my gatdamn belly.

SUTTER

Okay . . . We have to be sneaky about this.

OLD GRANNY

I can't be too gatdamn sneaky in this wheelchair.

SUTTER

I'm gonna get you some ribs but you have to promise not to
tell Mama.

OLD GRANNY

What the hell I need to tell your mama fo?

SUTTER

Alright.

(He works on his iPhone.
Old Granny watches.
After a moment:)

> OLD GRANNY

When you leavin to get the ribs?

> SUTTER

I'm doing it now.

> OLD GRANNY

The ribs down the street.

> SUTTER

I know.

> OLD GRANNY

You trying to tell me that the ribs gonna come out of that thing you got in your hand?

> SUTTER

Yes. Do you want short ribs?

> OLD GRANNY

I don't want no gatdamn short ribs I want my baby backs!

> SUTTER

Keep your voice down Granny . . . this has to be our secret . . .

> OLD GRANNY

(Whispers secret) I want my baby backs!!

> SUTTER

They got a baby backs and short ribs feast . . .

> OLD GRANNY

What the feast come with . . .

> SUTTER

A half slab of pork ribs and two chunks of beef ribs . . .

OLD GRANNY

Yeah give me that . . .

SUTTER

What sides you want?

OLD GRANNY

What they got?

SUTTER

Mashed potatoes.

OLD GRANNY

Yes.

SUTTER

Baked potatoes.

OLD GRANNY

Yes.

SUTTER

Sweet potato fries.

OLD GRANNY

That too.

SUTTER

Granny.

OLD GRANNY

Don't Granny me . . . I'm eighty-five gatdamn years old. Keep going.

SUTTER

Potato pancakes.

                              OLD GRANNY

Anything with potato in it. Get it.

                              SUTTER

Macaroni and cheese.

                              OLD GRANNY

Now we cookin.

                              SUTTER

Baked beans.

                              OLD GRANNY

Yes sweet Jesus. With some bacon in em.

                              SUTTER

Corn on the cob.

                              OLD GRANNY

Yes.

                              SUTTER

Creamed corn.

                              OLD GRANNY

Yes.

                              SUTTER

Cut sweet corn.

                              OLD GRANNY

Yes.

                              SUTTER

Onion rings.

OLD GRANNY

Mmm-hmm . . .

SUTTER

Grilled vegetables.

OLD GRANNY

Fuck I need some grilled vegetables for?

SUTTER

Steamed spinach.

OLD GRANNY

It got bacon in it.

SUTTER

I doubt it. Collard greens.

OLD GRANNY

BINGO!!!

SUTTER

Shh!! Granny . . .

OLD GRANNY

Put some bacon in them collards for me baby.

SUTTER

Alright . . . There . . . Done.

OLD GRANNY

What we do now?

SUTTER

We wait.

> OLD GRANNY

Ain't you gotta call em?

> SUTTER

No ma'am.

> OLD GRANNY

How they gonna know what we want?

> SUTTER

I just told them . . .

> OLD GRANNY

Oh . . . okay.

(Silence.)

You need my twenty dollars back?

> SUTTER

No. I already paid for it.

> OLD GRANNY

How you do that?

> SUTTER

You can do a lot of things with this Granny.

> OLD GRANNY

I guess so.

(Silence.)

So now we just wait?

> SUTTER

We just wait.

OLD GRANNY

We still gotta be sneaky?

SUTTER

Not as much . . .

OLD GRANNY

Okay . . .

(Silence.
Silence.
Silence.)

Sutter Boy.

SUTTER

Yes Granny?

OLD GRANNY

Do that dance that Michael Jackson useta lak to do . . .

(Silence.)

END OF PLAY

NOTE ON CURTAIN CALL

It is the playwright's wish that every production use their curtain call as a tribute to the LEGENDARY MICHAEL JACKSON. DANCE!!! DANCE!!! DANCE!!